T0194081

Other books by the author

Biff and Becka's Springtime Escapades

Biff and Becka's Stupendous Vacation

Biff and Becka's Splendiferous Christmas

Elaine's Kitchen Cookbook

JOURNAL GEMS

Nuggets from My Heart to Yours

ELAINE BEACHY

WESTBOW
PRESS®
A DIVISION OF THOMAS NELSON
& ZONDERVAN

Unless otherwise stated, all scripture taken from the New King James Version®. Copyright © 1982 by Thomas Nelson. Used by permission. All rights reserved.

Scripture quotations marked (NIV) are taken from the Holy Bible, New International Version®, NIV®. Copyright © 1973, 1978, 1984, 2011 by Biblica, Inc.™ Used by permission of Zondervan. All rights reserved worldwide. www. zondervan.com The "NIV" and "New International Version" are trademarks registered in the United States Patent and Trademark Office by Biblica, Inc.™

Scripture quotations marked (AMP) are taken from the Amplified Bible, Copyright © 1954, 1958, 1962, 1964, 1965, 1987 by The Lockman Foundation. Used by permission.

Scripture quotations marked (NLT) are taken from the Holy Bible, New Living Translation, copyright ©1996, 2004, 2015 by Tyndale House Foundation. Used by permission of Tyndale House Publishers, Inc., Carol Stream, Illinois 60188. All rights reserved.

WestBow Press books may be ordered through booksellers or by contacting:

WestBow Press
A Division of Thomas Nelson & Zondervan
1663 Liberty Drive
Bloomington, IN 47403
www.westbowpress.com
1 (866) 928-1240

ISBN: 978-1-9736-4150-6 (sc)
ISBN: 978-1-9736-4152-0 (hc)
ISBN: 978-1-9736-4151-3 (e)

Library of Congress Control Number: 2018911732

Print information available on the last page.

WestBow Press rev. date: 10/05/2018

Dedication

To Jesus, my Lord and Savior: may Your kingdom come, and Your will be done on earth, as it is in heaven! Thank You for my great salvation!

To my dear husband, children and grandchildren: your lives are a gift from God to me. I value our great family dynamic; thank you for your love expressed to me in so many ways. Thank you for encouraging me in my writing.

In memory of my dear father Edwin, and to my dear mother, Elva Yoder, my siblings, extended family and friends, thank you for your love and wonderful influence in my life.

To my faithful friends, Mary Ellen Caso, Sally Tomko, Joan Lubbe, Terry, and all the women of Deborah Company at Living Faith Church: thank you for your love and encouragement!

And to all who read this book:

Life can throw you a curve ball. That's when we all need hope and encouragement. My prayer is that as you read my "journal gems" I've written over the years, you will be taught, your heart will be lifted, and your hope renewed. May the Spirit of God breathe His presence into you; may you find the reading entertaining, inspiring, and life-changing. I bless you with excellent health, strength, long life, and good days, now and always, in Jesus' name. I bless you with a love for, and surrender to, the truth of God's word. God alone is your trustworthy guiding light for all of life's situations and troubles. Hold tightly to your faith in Jesus Christ; never be afraid to let your light shine!

Contents

1. Be Still 1

2. Two Chairs and a Journal.................................4

3. Making the Cut 7

4. Time Out..10

5. Talking to Trees 13

6. I Had A Dream 15

7. The Earth and You......................................18

8. Orlando 21

9. Matters of The Heart 24

10. The Gift of Friendship 27

11. To Pet the Cat..30

12. Communication.......................................33

13. Clutter 36

14. Doormats 39

15. Contentment...42

16. Kick the Hurry Habit..................................45

17. Birds and Barns.......................................48

18. How Does Your Garden Grow?.........................50

19. God is Good; the Devil is Bad 52

20. A Weapon Called Joy 55

21. What Do You Think? 58

22. Love Your Enemies...61

23. Pray for Your Children 63

24. Pass the Salt, Please 66

25. Sunsets and Anger..68

26. Soul Food..70

27. God Wants You Well...72

28. The Christmas Bonus...75

29. The Battle for the Mind 78

30. Love 81

31. Be Filled with the Holy Spirit.....................................84

32. Quiet, Please 87

33. The Dog Whisperer 90

34. Blessing Others 93

35. Love the Truth 96

36. Tiles and Shuttles 99

37. Old and New 102

38. Marriage Bedrock..105

39. Marriage Building..109

40. Love and Respect 112

41. A Softened Heart 116

42. Submission: A Dirty Word?.......................................119

43. Mirror, Mirror, on the Wall.......................................122

44. Sound Bites 125

45. Sex Matters 128

46. Giants and Grasshoppers..132

47. The Little White Church on Beachley Street.....................135

48. Loneliness 138

49. Why Work? 141

50. Celebrate Life 144

51. Haste Makes Waste 147

52. Masks 150

53. Holidays and Relationships 153

54. From Anger to Prayer 156

55. What Do You Say? 160

56. Thanksgiving 163

57. The Bait of Offense 166

58. To Give or Not to Give? That is the Question 169

59. Mothering Regrets 174

60. Renewing the Mind 177

PSALM 91 181

Scriptures and Declarations for Encouragement and Victory 183

Personal Note from the Author 187

Preface

There is a great need for every Christian to seriously read the Bible for themselves on a regular basis. Books and articles may all be well and good (and I have many), but nothing can take the place of God's word. In today's world, there are many voices that try to draw us away from what God really said. It's the age-old deception of the devil to whisper, "Did God really say?" as he did to Eve in the Garden of Eden. We must know exactly what God said.

Divided into sixty entries with Scriptures for meditation, *Journal Gems* is the result of Bible study over the years that reflects itself in my journaling and blogging. I write from a heart of love for God, for others, and a passion for the truth; I write to encourage, teach, and inspire. The only safeguard against deception by the enemy is to have a sincere love for God and the truth; we dare not prefer opinions based on feelings over the word of God. I pray you will find this book beneficial in your own life, and then let others know about it, too.

Be Still

Radio and TV stations are filled with so many voices that clamor for our attention. Riots, terrorism, sex trafficking, the drug trade, political intrigue, snarky behavior, betrayal, obstruction of truth, violence, and injustice threaten to overwhelm our nation and the world. Satan's gripping tentacles of moral decay seem to have made inroads everywhere—in the church, government, family, children caught in sexual confusion, elementary and high schools, halls of ivy, movies, video games, and music. And I am filled with righteous indignation.

I think of the biblical account of Lot who lived in the plains of Sodom and Gomorrah and what his life must have been like. Second Peter 2:7 - 8 tells us that God "delivered righteous Lot, who was oppressed by the filthy conduct of the wicked (for that righteous man, dwelling among them, tormented his righteous soul from day to day by seeing and hearing their lawless deeds)."

Sometimes, one tends to feel quite helpless and overwhelmed by the threat of such a world; the voices of fear and negativity are everywhere, and one's soul can all too easily undergo a negative osmosis.

When I sat down with my journal this morning, I sensed the Lord speaking to my heart: "Be still and know that I am God." I said, "Holy Spirit, talk to me about that." The following poem came to mind:

Be Still

Be still and know that I am God.

Do not worry; do not fret.
Those things you imagine
Have not happened yet.
Why borrow trouble? Why feel dismayed?
Fix your thoughts on good things—
I will come to your aid.

Be still and know that I am God.

Don't run here; don't run there,
Fighting just to beat the air.
Take your stand, as I have said.
You wear a crown upon your head.
Watch Me work. Look at Me;
It will change how you see.

Scripture to Meditate:

- "Therefore, humble yourselves under the mighty hand of God, that He may exalt you in due time, casting all your care upon Him, for He cares for you" (I Peter 5:7).
- Matthew 6:26 says, "Look at the birds of the air, for they neither sow nor reap nor gather into barns; yet your heavenly Father feeds them. Are you not of more value than they?"
- Read all of Psalm 37:1-11. God says, "Do not fret because of evildoers. . . Delight yourself also in the Lord and He shall give you the desires of your heart. . . Commit your way to the Lord, trust also in Him, and He shall bring it to pass . . . Rest in the

Lord, and wait patiently for Him; do not fret because of him who prospers in his way. . . The meek shall inherit the earth and shall delight themselves in the abundance of peace."

What is God speaking to your heart today?

_____

_____

Two Chairs and a Journal

From time to time, I pull out a chair across from me at the kitchen table and invite Jesus to sit and fellowship with me. I've found that personal invitation enhances the closeness I feel with my Lord and Savior. I ask the Holy Spirit to lead me in worship, prayer and conversation with Jesus.

After I pray in the Spirit, read and study the Bible, I tell Him what's on my mind—whether it's a solution I need, or just sharing my feelings. I want to be brutally honest with myself and with God. I have often prayed, "God, always give me a love for the truth, no matter what it is, no matter if it hits me and I need to change my thinking or behavior. I want to live a life based on honesty with You, myself, and others." He knows my thoughts and feelings anyway, and it's healthy to unload my burdens on Him.

One morning I asked Him, "Jesus, is there anything You want to say to me?" I wrote our conversation in my journal. The words I wrote down could just as well apply to the church of Jesus Christ.

Jesus to me: "You honor Me by walking in integrity of heart. I appreciate your love for the truth; you will be kept from deception.

"I have heard, and am answering, your prayers for your family. You have decreed divine order, and so it shall be established. I will make the crooked places straight, and the rough places a plain. I will strengthen you and uphold you; I will put My words in your mouth, and no one can stand against them. Every high thing shall come down; every stronghold shall be broken in answer to your prayers, for the sake of My covenant.

"Righteousness shall be exalted in this land once again. My truth shall occupy the public square, and many shall be turned from giving ear to the devil's lies and shall embrace the truth. Many shall turn to Me and be saved. I rejoice to see the fruit of My suffering! You make my heart glad, and I rejoice because you have accepted a holy warrior spirit given by Me! I will do great things through you—things you do not even know yet. I keep My word; you will not be disappointed, because you hope in Me!

"Do not be distraught over negative things you see and hear, for I am at work in America, in My church, and your family. Be at peace, my sister; I fight for you. The battle is Mine. Wear the shoes of peace I have given you and stand your ground. Do not be moved off My word or promises, for they shall surely come to pass."

Me: "Thank You, Jesus, for encouraging me. I put on the shoes of peace, and walk in love and victory, holding high the sword of the Spirit, the word of God! I am more than a conqueror, because You have already won the battle against the enemy. I stand firmly in Your victory! You are my King forever! You are to be obeyed! Every knee shall bow, and every tongue shall declare that You alone are Lord!"

Scripture to Meditate:

- "Finally, my brethren, be strong in the Lord and in the power of His might. Put on the whole armor of God, that you may be able to stand against the wiles of the devil, for we wrestle not against flesh and blood, but against principalities, against powers, against the rulers of the darkness of this age, against spiritual wickedness in the heavenly places" (Ephesians 6:10-12).

- Read Ephesians 6: 13 – 18; the verses tell you of your armor to fight spiritual battles.

What do you want to say to the Lord today?

_____

_____

3

Making the Cut

I reflected on my recent decision to cut some things out of my busy life—too busy, per my heavenly Father's words. And He was right. He has been at work in my heart to come aside from the hustle and bustle of "could and should." Besides the normal busyness of keeping the gears of my household well-oiled, I'm also publishing a cookbook (2016), writing a blog, interacting on social media, attending Women's Life every Tuesday and leading a small group with my husband at church early Sunday mornings. I have been attending three writer's group meetings per month, and don't even work outside the home, like many women do in this high-pressure, traffic-clogged, northern Virginia area.

I've talked to some stressed-out women who would also like to simplify their lives, but say they fear disappointing or angering others. They say they would miss their friends too much, or believe if they quit, things would fall apart at their church or for their friends. I can relate, because I used to be there, too. I have decided that everything doesn't depend on me. I hope they find the courage as well to make a cut where necessary.

My mind went to a poem I wrote in 2011; does this poem describe you?

Diary of a Mad Housewife

Clean the house, scrub the floor,
Wipe those smudges off the door.
Do the laundry, take out trash,
Clean the sink, then make a dash
To the grocery store, and then
Come back home and call a friend.

"My life's so busy," you complain;
"My husband really is a pain!
My kids—they drive me up a wall.
I don't like my life at all!
It's time for me; where's my career?
I want fulfillment—can't you hear?

My life's a mess. What did you say?
I gotta run—I can't delay.
I'll miss that sale at T.J. Maxx
If I don't hurry up and act!
Run, run, run, that's all I do.
I wonder where I put my shoes. . ."

Let me counsel this harried housewife to stop; forget her shoe
search, turn off her cell phone, turn off the television, radio, or whatever
else she's got going on, and reach for her Bible. I'd tell her to quiet her
mind, ask her heavenly Father some questions, and let Him talk to her.
He has all the answers, you know.

May you experience peace and quiet as Father draws your heart
toward home.

Scripture to Meditate:

- "For thus says the Lord God, the Holy One of Israel: 'In returning and rest you shall be saved; in quietness and confidence shall be your strength'" (Isaiah 30:15).
- "Repent [change your mind] therefore and be converted, that your sins may be blotted out, so that times of refreshing may come from the presence of the Lord" (Acts 3:19).

What are some things you need to cut out of your life?

_____

_____

4

Time Out

A good friend of mine introduced me to the book, *2 Chairs* by Bob Beaudine, and I recommend it to all. Sometimes the Christian discipline of a daily quiet time with the Lord can seem a bit stale and predictable, sort of like a marriage relationship that gets into the rut of daily routine. A new experience or change of scenery is invigorating and life-changing! The same goes for our most important relationship with our Lord and Savior.

As I pulled out a kitchen chair and took my place on the opposite side, I sensed my Lord's distinct pleasure as I invited Him to meet with me. I opened my Bible to Proverbs 4, and my heart responded with warmth as I read His words: "My child, pay attention to what I say. . . for they bring life and healing to your whole body. . . guard your heart above all else for it determines the course of your life. . . avoid perverse talk. . . look straight ahead. . . mark out a straight path for your feet. . . don't get sidetracked. . . keep your feet from following evil."

Then I sensed Him say to me, "The Old Testament tells you what is right and good, but the New Testament empowers you to obey through the Holy Spirit.

I asked Him to empower me to be obedient in a certain area I was praying about, and then I asked Him, "Jesus, is there anything You want to say to me today?"

Immediately I sensed His thoughts: "Bless Me, and I will make you a blessing!"

Because of church songs I'd sung growing up, I always thought He does all the blessing. So, I asked, "How can I bless You?"

This thought came to mind instantly: "Be thankful unto Him and bless His name." That was it! I bless Him by being thankful! Thank Him for who He is, what He has done for me and everyone. I bless Him by telling Him what I love about Him!

I told Him how great He is and thanked Him that He has forgiven all my sins, healed all my diseases, redeemed my life from the pit, crowned me with love and compassion, filled my mouth with good things, and renewed my youth like the eagle's (from Psalm 103). I thanked Him for His great love and sacrifice for me, for His pain and suffering, and for His victory over the thief, the devil. I thanked Him for my inheritance through His name, and for His word. I thanked Him for my earthly blessings of family, friends, church, nation, for law and order. There are so many things to thank Him for!

Besides saying, "I bless You, Lord," I bless Him by my obedience and thanksgiving, too. He feels loved and respected when I obey and thank Him. He knows what makes me feel loved as well.

A daily "time out" is vital to a happy, healthy spiritual relationship with Jesus. "Look! I stand at the door and knock. If you hear My voice and open the door, I will come in, and we will share a meal together as friends" (Revelation 3:20, New Living Translation).

Dear reader, He's there for you, too, in your "2-chair" moments, as an all-wise, all-knowing friend who loves you more than you ever dreamed possible. I also think it's important to value what He tells us by writing it down in a journal. You may be amazed at the thoughts you start picking up from Him once you put pen to paper. His thoughts never violate Scripture. He always encourages, comforts, exhorts, edifies and builds up just as He tells us to do when we prophesy to one another, as instructed in First Corinthians 14:3, 31.

How is God speaking to you?

_____

_____

5

Talking to Trees

In the shower one morning, the scripture from Mark 11:22 – 24 came to mind: "Have faith in God. For assuredly I say to you, whoever says to this mountain, 'Be removed and be cast into the sea,' and does not doubt in his heart, but believes that those things he says will be done, he will have whatever he says. Therefore, I say to you, whatever things you ask when you pray, believe that you receive them, and you will have them."

What prompted Jesus' words was His disciples' amazement to see that the fig tree Jesus cursed the day before was now dead: "Now in the morning, as they passed by, they saw the fig tree dried up from the roots. And Peter, remembering, said to Him, 'Rabbi, look! The fig tree which You cursed has withered away" (Mark 11:12 – 14). Jesus answered that whoever speaks likewise, will have the same results.

Our country has been on my heart so much lately. As I thought about these scriptures, and the current condition of violence in America, the words, "tree of violence" came to mind. I began to declare: "You tree of violence, I say to you, 'Be plucked up by the roots and be thrown into the sea, in Jesus' name! Every structure, plan, plot, organized effort, every vow, every subversive attempt to destroy our nation's law and order, be pulled out by the roots, and wither away! May no one ever eat of your fruit again! Close the mouths of the lions, Father! Send out Your angels of peace across America!'"

That tree of violence has many roots, but it shall lose its footing.

Later, at the kitchen table, I pulled out a chair for Jesus to come fellowship with me. I was praying in the Holy Spirit about these things, when I suddenly became aware that Jesus was praying with me for America!

I began to weep as we prayed together. Still weeping, I spoke to Jesus, "Let's just bless the Father!" I lifted my hands and worshiped Him. I sensed Him say to me, "Your prayers have been heard; you have what you requested." I responded, "May Your kingdom come, may Your will be done, on earth, as it is in Heaven! Amen."

What mountains need moving in your life right now?

_____

_____

6

I Had A Dream

One night in my dream, I was with my husband, Dave, at a small gathering of some kind, like a casual picnic. As people talked to one another, I felt the authority of the Spirit of God rise in me. I stood up, and announced, "Listen, folks, you need to be more concerned about your eternal destiny, than about who will be your next president!"

I cried out, "Jesus is Lord! Jesus is Lord! He is King of the world, and all are to worship Him! Do you know where you will spend eternity? Ask Jesus to forgive you of your sins and tell Him you receive Him as your Lord and Savior!"

One woman immediately came up to me and asked, "Would you please pray for me?"

As I moved to do so, with Dave next to me, others too crowded around, wanting me to pray for them. Soon a long line, as far as I could see, formed for prayer. I felt overwhelmed by the massive hunger of the people before me, and the opportunity it presented to be used of God. I remember thinking, "I need others to help me." Just as I started to pray for the woman, I awoke.

I prayed, "Lord Jesus, what do you want me to do? How can I pray for all these people?" I decided one way I can share the gospel of salvation through Jesus Christ is through my writing. Why the need for salvation, and what do I mean by that?

When man disobeyed God in the Garden of Eden, sin entered the world, bringing spiritual and physical death. Man lost fellowship with God. But God had a marvelous, self-sacrificing plan to restore fellowship with us, His dearly loved ones. He sent Jesus, His only Son, born of a virgin into the earth, to make payment for our sins by dying on the cross in our place. We deserved punishment because of our rebellion against God, but Jesus absorbed all God's anger against sin. Jesus died, was buried, but arose from the grave on the third day! And after being seen by many people over a period of some days, ascended into heaven and sat down at God's right hand, mission completed. Then God sent the Holy Spirit into the earth on the day of Pentecost to influence the heart of man to turn to God for salvation.

Now is the day of God's wonderful grace and favor! All you need do is accept the forgiveness of Jesus, and you will be saved from an eternity in hell without God. If you choose to reject God's free grace, the devil would still claim you, and God can't do anything about it. There are no second chances. Once you pass from this life, your destiny is sealed. It's up to you—it's your choice.

Will you respond to God's love for you? Please don't delay; accept God's love and forgiveness through Jesus Christ. If you do, you will never be judged for your sin, and you will be free from the devil's ownership of you. That's awesome news! What a gift from God!

Romans 10:9 – 10 assures us, "If you confess with your mouth the Lord Jesus and believe in your heart that God raised Him from the dead, you will be saved, for with the heart one believes unto righteousness, and with the mouth confession is made unto salvation."

My friend, wherever you are, you can bow your head, and pray something like this: "Jesus, thank You for dying on the cross and paying the price for my sins. I repent of all my sins and ask You to save me; I receive your free salvation, and I believe God raised You from the dead. Come into my life and give me everlasting life. I say you are my Lord and Savior from now on. Thank You for saving me, Jesus! Amen."

If you sincerely prayed that prayer, you are now born again by the Spirit of God and will escape the coming judgment on the earth! Read the Bible, especially the New Testament, beginning with the book of John. Jesus will lead and guide you into all truth. Talk to Him by faith (that means even though you can't see Him). He will help you with everything. Ask Him to fill you with His Holy Spirit, to lead you to a good Bible-believing church, and to give you Christian friends. These steps are very important to growing in the grace and knowledge of the Lord. Tell another Christian that you gave your life to Jesus; it will strengthen you. I'd love to hear from you, too, and tell me about your experience with Jesus.

Scripture to Meditate:

- "For all have sinned and fall short of the glory of God" (Romans 3:23).
- "For God so loved the world (that includes you!) that He gave His only begotten Son, that whoever believes in Him should not perish but have everlasting life" (John 3:16).
- "The Lord. . . is longsuffering toward us, not willing that any should perish but that all should come to repentance" (2 Peter 3:9).
- "Therefore, having been justified by faith, we have peace with God through our Lord Jesus Christ" (Romans 5:1).

Write out your prayer for salvation or thanksgiving to God for His love.

_____

_____

7

The Earth and You

"The earth is the Lord's, and all its fullness, the world and those who dwell therein" (Psalm 24:1). Then again, God says in Psalm 115:16, "The heaven, even the heavens, are the Lord's, but the earth He has given to the children of men." This reiterates what the Lord told Adam and Eve in Genesis 1:28: "Then God blessed them, and said to them, 'Be fruitful and multiply; fill the earth and subdue it; have dominion over the fish of the sea, over the birds of the air, and over every living thing that moves on the earth.'"

The meaning of the word "subdue" in Hebrew in Strong's Concordance is "To tread down; to conquer; subjugate, keep under, subdue, bring into subjection." One definition of "subdue" in Webster's Ninth New Collegiate Dictionary is "to bring under cultivation." That makes a lot of sense to me, for Adam was to have children who would have children to have dominion over the earth, which includes cultivating to grow food and take care of the earth. God's desire for mankind is that "everyone shall sit under his vine and under his fig tree, and no one shall make them afraid" (Micah 4:4).

Television minister Charles Capps said he caught a lot of fish while on a fishing trip with a friend, but his buddy complained he hadn't caught any. They both had a good laugh when Charles told him, "The

Lord said I have dominion over the fish of the sea, so I tell those fish to come to me, and they do! It works!" I believe we have authority in Jesus' name over the animals, even in dangerous situations with them.

We do not own the world: God does. However, He has clearly made us caretakers of the earth, and we are responsible and accountable for how we use it. He has given us all things richly to enjoy (I Timothy 6:17), and we must be good stewards of our planet. However, we are not to worship the earth and call nature "God." We must make reasonable use of all God has given: oil, gas, coal, trees, water, minerals in the earth, etc. Man is to rule the earth—the earth is not to rule mankind. Some legislative regulations wrongly make the earth superior to man and severely curtail the earth's potential.

Nature is so beautiful and complex and speaks of God, our great Creator. Psalm 19:1 says, "The heavens declare the glory of God, and the firmament shows His handiwork." Who of us has not marveled at the sight of a glorious sunset or sunrise? At all kinds of trees, birds, flowers, animals and insects of all kinds? We are so thankful for fruits and vegetables, fresh, clean water in lakes, rivers and streams. The ocean holds all kinds of creatures, and the mountains boast of hidden treasures of diamonds, gold, fossil fuel and oil for mankind to use. God has provided us with everything we need, such as a wide variety of trees for building homes, making furniture and beautiful things. He has given people wisdom and many creative ideas that are to be used to benefit mankind—not just themselves.

As stewards of the earth, we must not ravage, pillage, or abuse our resources, but take care of them. For example, the farmer must put nutrients back into the earth after he has grown his crops, so the soil is not depleted. We have game wardens to monitor hunting and wildlife, and service rangers to preserve our national parks. We guard against soil erosion and pollution of our air, waterways and oceans.

On a personal level, it is a godly thing to have neat, clean homes, manicured lawns and landscaping. We are thankful for sanitation system, recycling and weekly garbage pick-up, for workers that sweep our streets, and pick up trash along the highways. Our daughter and son-in-law have made it a habit to pick up trash every time they go for a walk. We can all do our part in being good stewards of the earth. It's a godly thing indeed!

Scripture to Meditate:

"For the earnest expectation of the creation eagerly waits for the revealing of the sons of God. For the creation was subjected, not willingly, but because of Him who subjected it in hope; because the creation itself also will be delivered from the bondage of corruption into the glorious liberty of the children of God. For we know that the whole creation groans and labors with birth pangs together until now" (Romans 8:19 – 22)

How can you improve on taking care of your part of the earth?

_____

_____

Orlando

Anytime a human tragedy strikes, there are always diverse voices that claim to know the reason why. Such has been the case since creation of time. Adam blamed his wife, Eve, for the tragedy of disobedience that led to their eviction from Eden, the Garden of God. Eve blamed the serpent for beguiling her with smooth talk. (Who said, "Sticks and stones may break my bones, but words will never hurt me?")

There are some people who declare that the forty-nine killed and the fifty-three injured inside the gay bar, Pulse, in Orlando, Florida, on June 12, 2016, was the consequence of their own sin of homosexual behavior. They seem to be saying those people deserved to die. But I ask you, if that is true, how many of us would be alive today for sins we've committed? We all deserve to die for our sins, but Jesus paid the debt we owed God when He died for us and arose from the dead. No, I don't believe it was God's judgment on those people. I believe God wept when they were murdered. My heart is filled with pain as I wonder where those souls are now. "God is not willing that any should perish, but that all should come to repentance" (2 Peter 3:9).

I also think it's despicable that some try to raise funds and make political hay from this and other tragedies. They fall back on erroneous worn-out rhetoric, saying if guns were outlawed in the United States, the killing would stop. Really? I beg to differ. Criminals and terrorists will always be able to find weapons on the black market. Are we to ban the making of all guns, swords, knives (kitchen knives too), and sling shots? Consider: countless tools, including rocks, pillows, baseball bats, bricks, poison, glass, and so forth, ad nauseam, can be weapons of murder—including the human hand.

I contend with every fiber of my being that the root of the issue is not the weapon: it is the condition of sin in the human heart. No one can change the heart except Jesus Christ through the power of the Holy Spirit. Jeremiah 17:9 states, "The heart is deceitful above all things and beyond cure. Who can understand it?" What happened in Orlando was not the judgment of God. It was the evil in the hearts of the killers who did the will of their master, Satan, who comes to steal, kill, and destroy.

I think of Jesus' words to His disciples when the Samaritans wouldn't welcome them on their way to Jerusalem. "And when His disciples James and John saw this, they said, 'Lord, do you want us to command fire to come down from heaven and consume them, just as Elijah did?' But He turned and rebuked them, and said, 'You do not know what manner of spirit you are of. For the Son of Man did not come to destroy men's lives but to save them'" (Luke 9:54-56).

Jesus also said in Luke 13:4, "Or those eighteen who died when the tower in Siloam fell on them—do you think they were more guilty than all the others living in Jerusalem? I tell you, no. But unless you repent, you too will all perish."

I rejoiced when I heard how Chick-fil-A, at the time of the horrendous attack at the gay bar, showed Christ's love by opening their restaurant that Sunday (they are never open on Sundays), and distributed free sandwiches and iced tea to those standing in line for hours to donate blood for the wounded. They also served hundreds of law enforcement officials who were at the scene of the murders. That's something Jesus would do—not call down fire on a gay night club.

Scripture to Meditate:

- "The thief does not come except to steal, and to kill, and to destroy. I have come that they may have life, and that they may have it more abundantly" (John 10:10).
- "Out of the heart come evil thoughts, murder, adultery, sexual immorality, theft, false testimony and slander" (Matthew 15:19).
- "For from within, out of men's hearts, come evil thoughts, sexual immorality, theft, murder, adultery, greed, malice, deceit, lewdness, envy, slander, arrogance and folly. All these evils come from inside and make a man unclean" (Mark 7:21 – 23)

What changes do you want to make in your attitude toward sinful people?

_____

_____

9

Matters of The Heart

This is a time of great upheaval in America. Common sense, decency, and morality seem eclipsed by scathing vitriol against Christians and conservative leadership of any kind in our country. Where is the respect and good will that can result in good decisions for our country when both sides of the political aisle come together?

A great challenge confronts me as a Christian with biblically-informed political beliefs and an innate, deep-seated sense of justice, to obey the words of Jesus in Matthew 5:44-45: "But I say to you, love your enemies; bless those who curse you, do good to those who hate you, and pray for those who spitefully use you and persecute you, that you may be the sons of your Father in heaven; for He makes His sun rise on the evil and on the good, and sends rain on the just and the unjust."

My heart wrestles with the challenge: how can I bless those who do such evil? How should I bless them? God's Kingdom works in an upside-down fashion from the kingdoms of this world, to bring things right-side-up. I realize I need to guard my own heart, so I am not sucked down into the sewer of destructive thinking that wars against the Holy Spirit's will.

One can see from the scripture mentioned above that God is a "blesser." He desires for all people to be saved and come to the knowledge of the truth. In the book, *The Power of Blessing* by Kerry Kirkwood, I read numerous testimonies of how God turned people's hearts around when the offended ones chose to bless those opposing them. I took courage from that, and the Holy Spirit showed me that as I imitate God by blessing the difficult or ungodly, I humble myself to bless rather than hold resentment and bitterness against them. As I bless them, God can move in and change obstinate hearts.

I do not bless the actions of a person; rather, I pray something like this: "Father, in Jesus' name, I bless _____ with showers of Your love; I bless their eyes to be opened, so they can come to the truth. I bless them with health, strength, righteousness, long life and good days. I bless their hearts to be impacted by Your grace. Amen."

What would happen if the entire body of Christ made blessing our enemies a priority in our lives? If we truly obeyed 2 Chronicles 7:14? "If My people who are called by My name will humble themselves, and pray and seek My face, and turn from their wicked ways, then I will hear from heaven, and will forgive their sin and heal their land."

I want to do what I can to cultivate a culture of blessing within the body of Christ. With it, we can change the world, one heart at a time! Think of the peace that would come to our nation and the nations of the world. Blessing our enemies is powerful. Anyone can bless those who agree with them, but it takes a humbling of the heart to do it for our enemies. We must let go of offense and view others as God sees them: souls for whom Jesus died. Think of the eternal consequences if they don't repent and turn to God. We plead for their salvation. We must have the heart of God for our world, and not be sucked down by it. And when I choose the pathway of blessing, peace comes into my own heart in great measure, and I know God can now work on changing them.

Will you be part of a culture of blessing? Maybe you want to start with those difficult people in your own family.

God, give us grace to be a people of blessing. I press on, daily.

Scripture to Meditate:

- "Therefore, I exhort first of all that supplications, prayers, intercessions, and giving of thanks be made for all men, for kings and all who are in authority, that we may lead a quiet and peaceable life in all godliness and reverence. For this is good and acceptable in the sight of God our Savior, who desires all men to be saved and to come to the knowledge of the truth" (I Timothy 2:1 – 4).

- "And let us not grow weary while doing good, for in due season we shall reap if we do not lost heart" (Galatians 6:9).
- "Not returning evil for evil or reviling for reviling, but on the contrary, blessing, knowing that you were called to this, that you may inherit a blessing" (I Peter 3:9).

What enemies will you bless today? List them here.

_____

_____

10

The Gift of Friendship

Some time ago as Mom and I talked, we got onto the subject of friendship. I learned that when she was a fourteen-year-old girl in school, she and nine other girls formed a circle of friendship that has remained intact to this day, seventy-eight years later! I was astounded. As I questioned her, she said as teenagers, they started writing a circle letter, and have faithfully kept it going all these years. Of the ten, there are only three friends still living.

In a circle letter, someone in the group writes a letter, and sends it to the next person on her list in the group, then that person writes a letter, includes the first person's letter, and sends it to the third person, and so on. (That must have been a fat envelope by the time it got around to all ten members!) When it comes around to the person who started the circle, she takes out her original letter, writes a new one, and sends it on again. (That was a long-hand version of social media!)

The fact that these faithful friends kept the circle letter going speaks of great commitment to that friendship. As years, weddings, births, deaths, states and miles separated them, they kept writing. Mom's voice filled with emotion as she related how two of her friends' husbands had died, and how the pen pals came together in a show of support at the funerals.

Lasting friendship is a gift from God. We all need friends to encourage us, pray for us, understand us, and believe in us. Friendships need to be nurtured, or they will wither and die. Here are some H A N G U P S that will kill a friendship:

- Hostility over Scripture interpretation
- Accusations
- Needing to be right about everything
- Gossip—betrayal of a confidence
- Unforgiving attitude
- Political arguments
- Selfishness

Dear Pooh Bear, that storybook character loved by so many, was an encourager. He has much to teach us about friendship. The soft-spoken, patient, forbearing, forgiving, honey-loving, lovable-ball-of-fluff-Pooh is so endearing. Even when he eats too much and gets stuck in Rabbit's hole. (Rabbit is not quite as charitable). And who can forget Eyeore, that down-in-the-mouth, always-seeing-the-glass-half-empty donkey? Then there was Tigger. "Bouncy, trouncy, flouncy, pouncy, full of fun, fun, fun! The wonderful thing about Tiggers is, I'm the only one!" (He had a bit of trouble with reality, as I recall.) Pooh never condemned him— only loved him. "Chubby little cubby all stuffed with fluff" serves as a good role model for friendship.

"Anxiety in the heart of man causes depression, but a good word makes it glad" (Proverbs 12:25). It's refreshing to have someone stick up for you when you feel beaten down, and someone to help you up when you fall. Being with a good friend brings warmth to a soul chilled by the winds of adversity. However, sometimes being a good friend is hard when you must tell them the truth in love. Take comfort in Proverbs 27:6 that says, "Faithful are the wounds of a friend, but the kisses of an enemy are deceitful."

Scripture to Meditate:

- "A man who has friends must himself be friendly. But there is a friend who sticks closer than a brother" (Proverbs 18:24).
- "Two are better than one, because they have a good reward for their labor. For if they fall, one will lift up his companions. But woe to him who is alone when he falls, for he has no one to help him up. Again, if two lie down together, they will keep warm; but how can one be warm alone? Though one may be overpowered by another, two can withstand him" (Ecclesiastes 4:9 – 12).

What can you do to nurture your friendships?

_____

_____

11

To Pet the Cat

For years, our adult son, Doug, longed to own a cat, and got excited as he finally chose a female Russian Blue he named *Saya*, and filled out the paperwork at the pet shelter. Anticipation mounted as he (and we) talked about all the fun he would have with her.

He bought all sorts of cat supplies: a cat carrier, an elaborate cat tree with all the "bells and whistles," a cat scratching post, cat bed, bowls for food and water, automated litter box, wet and dry cat food, cat toys, and even catnip. He did a lot of research online about cat care and joined a chat group about cats.

He chose his guest room as the initiation station for Saya, because he knew from what the shelter (and others) told him, that cats can take weeks to become acclimated to their new surroundings, and he wanted to make the transition as easy for her as possible. He lifted the bedspread on all sides, so he could peer under the guest bed to see her. He put water and food bowls on old towels on the floor and positioned her litter box away from the eating area and put some toy mice on the floor.

The big day finally arrived, and he brought her home. (The shelter told Doug it took three people to get her into the pet carrier!) Poor Saya. He set the carrier on the floor in his guest room, opened the door of the carrier slowly, and talked to her in low, gentle tones. She refused to leave the carrier and stayed frozen in place. When he checked later, the carrier was empty. After searching with a flashlight, he found her hiding under the bed. Saya didn't eat or use the litter box for two days. He went into her room every morning, knelt on the carpet where she could see him, and opened a can of cat food, put it in her bowl, gave her fresh water, and walked out. He put pheromone air plug-ins in the guest room that are designed to make the cat feel at ease.

Because he was concerned about her welfare, Doug bought two video cameras and installed them in strategic places to catch her movements. He hoped and watched for her to leave the hiding place under the bed and venture out, glad when he saw she'd eaten food, drunk water, and used the litter box. Day after day passed. One week moved into the next with little change. We prayed for Saya to become acclimated to her new home.

Since Doug works from home as a senior software engineer, he decided to sit on the floor with his laptop near the doorway of Saya's room every morning to help her get used to him. But she refused to budge. We encouraged Doug, saying that one of these days, she will learn to trust him.

Then, on the 28th day, almost four weeks to the day after he brought her home, it happened! His eyes filled with tears as he told us, "Today I petted my cat!" We hugged one another in celebration. He sent us video camera footage later of the happy event of him lying on the floor in her room as he held out his hand to Saya. She came to him and rubbed her head against his hand, walked alongside his body and let him stroke her spine, tail straight up in the air.

I had to think of spiritual parallels to the Saya saga: how God woos us to come to Him, trust Him, relate to Him, and be friends with Him. So often people have life and "pre-rescue" issues that make it hard to do that. Aren't you glad God is patient and understanding, and provides others to help us have faith in Him? I am.

I think of the scripture verse in Psalm 103:14. "For He knows our frame; He remembers that we are dust." Even after we have been rescued by Him from Satan's grasp, many of us have difficulty trusting Him. We are used to self-protection and self-preservation. Many of us have been made to feel afraid of making a misstep in our Christian walk, afraid of being judged by God, so we draw back from Him and try to hide. We've been made to feel guilty by religious teaching instead of being established in righteousness and grace. He understands our insecurities and wounds, and longs to befriend and heal us. God waits for us to respond to Him. He is a gentleman and will not force Himself on anybody. James 4:8 says, "Draw near to God, and He will draw near to you."

Jesus holds out His hand to each of us and says, "Come to Me, all you who labor and are heavy laden, and I will give you rest. Take My yoke upon you and learn from Me, for I am gentle and lowly in heart, and you will find rest for your souls. For my yoke is easy, and My burden is light" (Matthew 11:28-30). He's waiting patiently with a heart full of longing and love for your response. Will you come to Him? Will you let Him touch your heart? You can trust Him.

Identify an area in your life where you have difficulty trusting God. Then ask the Holy Spirit to comfort you. He is a faithful friend!

_____

_____

12

Communication

We develop trust (or distrust) from the time we're born. As babies, when we were hungry, cold, wet, tired, or in pain, we expressed that need through crying. A parent picked us up, the need was addressed, and trust established. Dr. Spock's seriously flawed theory was that one should just let the child cry so as not to "spoil" him. That can start a cycle of mistrust if we're left to cry for long periods of time. We learn it's painful to not have our needs met when we voice them.

Then as we grow up, we close our heart (and mouth) because we're afraid people will reject us. We don't "cry" any more. Our relationships become superficial. We think, "If they really knew what I thought our how I feel, they wouldn't like me." Or we may lash out with criticism and judgement that says, "I'm keeping you away from me. It hurts to not have my needs met."

I have read that when we learn to not have our needs met, we develop an orphan spirit. And from that orphan spirit, one turns to something to have that need met, such as sexual promiscuity, homosexual tendencies, alcohol, drugs, pornography, addictions, etc. Everyone needs to feel connected, safe, and loved. I find Gary Chapman's book on the Five Love Languages very helpful for spouses, family and friends, to find out and communicate what makes them feel loved.

The good news is that Jesus promised, "I will not leave you as orphans" (John 14:18). He will heal every heart hurt if we come to Him with it. He says, "Forgive all the people who've hurt you; trust Me, and I will heal your every hurt." Don't ever close your heart to anyone. Boundaries may need to be established so others will not abuse us, but our hearts can still be open to them as we pray God's best for them. (But it doesn't mean we have to hang out with them). If we trust God to heal every heart hurt, our identity will change; we'll feel strong.

Instead of telling someone, "You are so controlling," or "You are so rude," it's much better to honestly say, "When you do/say that, I feel hurt (or angry, threatened, whatever the case may be). Make it about how you feel. That way, the other person gets to decide how to respond to you. If you said, "You're so controlling," it would be a hostile expression toward the other person, and likely cause communication to shut down. It's always right to say how you feel, in a respectful way.

Have you ever been around someone where you could feel the emotional tension, but they wouldn't talk? When you asked them what's wrong, they replied, "Nothing." Yet, they want you to figure out what they're so upset about. Maybe you've been such a person. Many people lack life skills needed for good communication.

Learn to express yourself—your needs. Don't expect your needs to be noticed by someone else. Sometimes we think people should be able to read our minds. But my responsibility is to know what is going on inside of me and express it. You are responsible to know what's going on inside of you and express it. I am not responsible to know what's going on inside of you. You're responsible to communicate your need to me.

Why don't we say what we mean? Why don't we say how we feel? I believe the answer is fear of rejection. Speaking the truth in love will always work. God's kind of love never fails. 2 Timothy 1:7 says, "For God has not given us a spirit of fear, but of power, and of love, and of a sound mind."

Scripture to Meditate:

- "When my mother and father forsake me, then the Lord will take care of me" (Psalm 27:10).
- "What then shall we say? If God is for us, who can be against us? He who did not spare His own Son, but delivered Him up for us all, how shall He not with Him freely give us all things" (Romans 8:31 – 33)?

Where can you let God help you with the trust factor in your communication?

_____

_____

Clutter

We've probably all watched a television show about hoarders. But clutter isn't confined to just our personal "stuff" in the home.

In emotional clutter, a person whose loved one has died may find it difficult to throw things away because of the need to keep feeling a love connection. I think a good solution that honors their memory is to take pictures of everything and place them neatly in a scrap book. Or some people may prefer to sell some of their own items and keep their loved ones' treasures.

Some people keep "helpful" clutter just in case a neighbor needs to borrow one of the ten drills hubby stores in the garage. Or we keep things just in case we may ever need them. For example, we may keep clothes that are too small, hoping to someday get back into them. By the time we lose the weight (if ever), the style is outdated or no longer appeals to us. Our tastes in clothing do change over time. We can give away clothes we don't wear.

Some buy big houses and strain their budgets to keep up with the Joneses; we foolishly buy bigger houses with more rooms to store more "stuff." Beware: it can easily lead to credit card debt and financial clutter.

A burgeoning calendar of activities is another form of clutter. We can buy a calendar with bigger squares to write more "stuff" on it, but we each only get twenty-four hours in a day. We can learn to say "no" to some activities, and instead, invest in time spent with our families. Above all, one needs to have quiet time with God, to meditate on His Word and pray.

Trashy speech is mouth clutter. Do we gossip, use profanity, or simply just talk too much? Have you ever been around someone who talks constantly? It wearies the soul. "Let your speech always be with grace, seasoned with salt, that you may know how you ought to answer each one" (Colossians 4:6).

Then there's intellectual clutter. We can be addicted to the stock market, news and politics, sports stats and scores, and follow movie stars or singers, etc. It's wise to curtail information overload. Constant controversy and arguments are also clutter.

Relationships can become cluttered too. Sometimes to preserve the boundaries of one's person-hood, it becomes necessary to set limits on the amount of access people have to one's life. Don't become a doormat, or a "yes-man/woman." Don't give of yourself or your finances out of obligation or compulsion. It will clutter your life with unhealthy emotions. Second Corinthians 9:7 says, "So let each one give as he purposes in his heart, not grudgingly or of necessity; for God loves a cheerful giver."

Scripture to Meditate:

- "But take heed to yourselves, lest your hearts be weighed down with carousing, drunkenness, and cares of this life, and that Day come on you unexpectedly" (Luke 21:34).
- "Laziness casts one into a deep sleep, and an idle person will suffer hunger" (Luke 19:15).
- "Let the words of my mouth and the meditation of my heart be acceptable in Your sight, O Lord, my strength and my Redeemer" (Psalm 19:14).

- "Let your speech always be with grace, seasoned with salt, that you may know how you ought to answer each one" (Colossians 4:6).
- "And I will walk at liberty, for I seek Your precepts" (Psalm 119:45).

Where can you leave clutter behind, and can say "yes" to a clean heart and home? God will help you make room to live life to the fullest!

_____

_____

Doormats

Do you feel like you must do what others expect of you? Can't say "no" to a request? Do you let people walk all over you? Are you afraid to disagree for fear it will sound unchristian? Sometimes people expect us to agree or be silent because we're Christians. After all, aren't we supposed to be kind and helpful and just love everybody? Aren't we supposed to avoid controversy? Aren't we supposed to put others first and ourselves last?

Maybe you have a "no" stuck on your tongue. Perhaps you feel powerless—always at the mercy of someone else's wishes or crisis. I used to be a powerless person; "yes" rolled off my tongue quite freely because I wanted people to think well of me. God forbid I should ever say "no" to a request or truly speak my mind. "Don't make waves, Elaine; keep the peace, just get along. Don't make anyone angry. Always accommodate others." No one told me to do that; it was just how I coped in life.

Now, don't get me wrong; I truly love people and like to help them. But I need to love myself too. Am I not as valuable as others? Scripture says in Mark 12:30 – 31: "And you shall love the Lord your God with all your heart, with all your soul, with all your mind, and with all your strength. This is the first commandment. And the second, like it, is this: 'You shall love your neighbor as yourself.'" Think about it: if I don't love and respect myself, how can I love and respect my neighbor?

People who take advantage of our generosity are takers and expect our compliance. Years ago, I was asked to fill in as leader of a kids' class on a Sunday night at church. The church leader assured me I would only need to do it until they found someone else—a week or two at the most. I gave up Sunday night plans with my family to accommodate his request. Several months went by before I finally approached him and complained that he'd not kept his word. I felt angry. He laughed a bit and said in a condescending tone, "Aw, did someone step on your widdle-bitty heart?" So, I told him, "I quit: I won't be there anymore." I was finished. I felt disrespected and taken advantage of. At the same time, I felt guilty, because, after all, wasn't this good church work for God? Was I right to not want to do it anymore? Yes, I was.

Sure, we want to be cheerful givers to our family, friends, and others. But if we end up feeling exploited, and don't confront takers, we can easily become offended and bitter. The way we can be a cheerful giver and protect our relationships is to let people know where our boundaries are. Then we can give because we want to, not because we must. If we don't have healthy boundaries, we can't give cheerfully, and others will not respect us because we don't respect ourselves. Our priorities, not the needs of others, should control our choices.

Why do we think it's somehow unloving or uncaring to be honest and tell people we don't have time for something, have other plans, or have no interest in doing what they asked? Just because we have good boundaries doesn't mean we are hard-hearted, or don't love people, either. Jesus Himself had good boundaries. Jesus said to His disciples in Mark 6:3, "'Come aside by yourselves to a deserted place and rest a while.' For there were so many coming and going, and they did not even have time to eat."

We can choose to be powerful and cheerful in our relationships rather than upset and powerless, always at the mercy of everyone else's opinions and desires. For more on this subject, I recommend the book, *Keep Your Love on,* by Danny Silk.

Scripture to Meditate:

- "So, let each one give as he purposes in his heart, not grudgingly or of necessity; for God loves a cheerful giver" (2 Corinthians 9:7).
- "Therefore, whatever you want men to do to you, do also to them, for this is the Law and the Prophets" (Matthew 7:12).
- "We should no longer be children, tossed to and fro and carried about with every wind of doctrine, by the trickery of men, in the craftiness of deceitful plotting, but speaking the truth in love, may grow up in all things into Him who is the Head—Christ" (Ephesians 4:14 – 15)

Do you feel like a doormat? If so, write how you plan to change that.

_____

_____

15

Contentment

Even as a senior citizen, I still love Veggie Tales! When I babysat our granddaughter years ago, she and I loved to watch Madame Blueberry and the Stuff Mart. Although Madame had lots of good friends and a nice tree house, she was still unhappy because she thought she needed more stuff.

Is it possible the reason we are discontent is because we're afraid someone else will get ahead of us, receive more praise or approval? The Lord says, "Your value is not in what you have, but in who I say you are."

You may ask, "Are you saying I shouldn't care what house I live in, what kind of clothes I have, or whether or not I have enough money?" No, that's not what I'm saying. God created us to be creative, invent things, and be a good care-taker of what He's given us. I like what I read somewhere: we shouldn't be discontent to the point of being agitated or disquieted.

If we so choose, the simple things in life bring us joy and contentment. Charles Dickens said, "Cheerfulness and contentment are great beautifiers and are famous preservers of youthful looks." Madame Blueberry certainly wasn't nice to be around when she was sucked into Complaining Swamp. In the end, she learned to be thankful for what she had.

Contentment comes from learning to be thankful—not comparing ourselves to others or entertaining the green-eyed monster. Comparisons create feelings of stress, envy, jealousy, and resentment. What does it matter if someone is smarter, cuter, has something nicer or bigger, or is approved by "high" society? Our worth does not depend on earthly, temporal things. As followers of Jesus Christ, our perspective must be on eternal values learned from God's word.

The Russian author, Leo Tolstoy, tells the story of a man who was told he could have all the land he could walk around in one day, but he had to be back at the starting point by sundown. The man walked for a long time, and thought he'd better head back, but he kept saying, "Just a little bit farther" and kept walking to widen his territory. Finally, he knew he had to head back, and he ran. In the distance he saw his starting place, and in a burst of speed and determination, he crossed the finish line just as the sun slipped behind the hill. He fell to the ground, gasping for breath, and died. In the end, the only land he needed was six feet.

Scripture to Meditate:

- "But godliness with contentment is great gain; for we brought nothing into this world, and we can take nothing out of it. But if we have food and clothing, we will be content with that" (I Timothy 6:6).

- "Keep your lives free from the love of money and be content with what you have, because God has said, 'Never will I leave you; never will I forsake you. So, we say with confidence, 'The Lord is my helper; I will not be afraid. What can man do to me?'" (Hebrews 13:5).

- "Command those who are rich in this present world not to be arrogant nor to put their hope in wealth, which is so uncertain, but to put their hope in God, who richly provides us with everything for our enjoyment. Command them to do good, to

be rich in good deeds, and to be generous and willing to share"
(I Timothy 6:17 – 18 NIV).

Tell the Lord what you are thankful for.

_____

_____

16

Kick the Hurry Habit

Harry let out a swear word as he yelled at the car ahead of him. "Get a move on, you creep; I haven't got all day!" He blew one long, loud blast on the horn as he moved within an inch of the offending car's rear bumper. The other driver stuck his hand out the window and gave Harry a not-so-nice hand signal.

"Good grief, Harry, calm down," his wife Melda admonished. "You'll give yourself a heart attack!" Harry gave Melda a withering glance, gripped the steering wheel, and retorted, "I don't want to be late for church!"

When we hurry, our muscle tension increases, blood pressure rises, and hormones are released that, if prolonged, hinder the body's healing and recovery processes. When we hurry, we work faster, lift heavier, and are accident-prone. My mom used to say, "Haste makes waste!" And it's so true; in our frustration to open flour and cereal bags, for example, they often rip open, and the contents spill everywhere. In our hurry, milk or water gets knocked over, and the stress to deal with the mess is worse than ever. Maybe we won't need to "cry over spilled milk" if we slow down and take our time.

And we eat too fast. Why? Sometimes it's because we oversleep and then need to gulp something for breakfast before we dash off to school, work, church, or an appointment. Sometimes it's just a habit. As a commercial construction superintendent, my husband said he learned to eat fast on the job site, because he had to coordinate the work of many subcontractors and often had to "eat on the run."

Hurry spills over into listening, too. We can easily get bored with people who speak slower or take their time to tell a story. Are we so proud as to think that what someone has to say is not worth our time? Do husbands and wives pay attention when their spouse talks? Do parents take time to listen patiently to their children who want to share something? Or are we so rushed in our schedules that our kids (and spouses) get lost in the shuffle? Children can feel devalued and unloved because parents don't take time to slow down, listen to them, and play with them.

Several years ago, I knew a lady who never answered her phone, but left a terse answering machine message: "We're busy—leave a message!" The word "busy" sounded like the punctuated buzz of a bee, and one was left with the impression she was even annoyed she took time to make the recording. When I was around her, she talked of all she had to do, all that was going on, and seemed to wear busyness like a badge of honor. I've come to realize that the more prominently a person wears that badge, the more disrespect and downright rudeness they display.

We hurry our quiet time with God—if we have one at all. This is an area I've had to work on. How easy it is to let the tyranny of the urgent supersede good intentions. I must train my mind to put things into perspective and make a quality decision to satisfy the desire of my spirit. When I do, I feel peaceful, de-stressed, satisfied, and the rest of the day goes so much better.

There is a big difference between being busy in an emergency and being habitually busy. Our bodies were not designed to be in a continual state of "fight or flight." We can choose different thoughts. We can learn to go to bed on time, get up on time, and begin our day with God. When we choose to be orderly, put things in their proper perspective, refuse to stress out over traffic lights, and deliberately slow down, we will notice a relaxed feeling of freedom in our bodies. We'll get back our sense of control and increase our overall energy level. We need to kick the hurry habit for our own wellbeing and for the sake of everyone around us.

Scriptures to Meditate:

- "My brethren, count it all joy when you fall into various trials, knowing that the testing of your faith produces patience. But let patience have its perfect work, that you may be perfect and complete, lacking nothing" (James 1:2 – 4).
- "But the fruit of the Spirit is love, joy, peace, longsuffering, kindness, goodness, faithfulness, gentleness, self-control. Against such there is no law" (Galatians 5:22).
- "The plans of the diligent lead surely to plenty, but those of everyone who is hasty, surely to poverty" (Proverbs 21:5).
- "Do you see a man hasty in his words? There is more hope for a fool than for him" (Proverbs 29:20).

Where do you need to kick the hurry habit?

_____

_____

17

Birds and Barns

Matthew 6:26 says, "Look at the birds of the air, for they neither sow nor reap nor gather into barns; yet your heavenly Father feeds them. Are you not of more value than they?"

You are so very special to God! If He provides for the little birds, how much more will He provide for you? What a comforting truth. God does not literally hand food to the birds but gives them instinct to search for food and find it. He's given them instinct on how to build their nests and provides the nesting material, but they must gather and build. God provides everything we need, too. He gives us inspired ideas and the desire to go after dreams and goals he's put into our hearts. He will not make us do anything, but He honors and trusts us to use all the blessings and resources He gives us.

God has promised provision for all our needs, and it comes in different ways. We watch for opportunities to present themselves, for doors to open. With faith and patience, we speak His promises into our situations and watch Him bring about what we need. We also want to look for ways we can bless others and not just think about ourselves and our needs. When we count our blessings, we find we are indeed richly blessed by God.

I think of the scripture in Second Peter 1:2 – 4 that says, "Grace and peace be multiplied to you in the knowledge of God and of Jesus our Lord, as His divine power has given us all things that pertain to life and godliness, through the knowledge of Him who called us by glory and virtue, by which have been given to us exceedingly great and precious promises, that through these you may be partakers of the divine nature, having escaped the corruption that is in the world through lust."

Scripture also says in Second Corinthians 1:20, "For all the promises of God in Him are Yes, and in Him Amen, to the glory of God through us." We agree with and stand on the promises God has made so that we may have what He has promised. Just as birds search for food, we need to search the word of God for spiritual food, so we can build our proverbial house on the Rock (See Matthew 7:24 – 27). We want to read God's word, so we will come to know the goodness of God. God will provide; He will give you wisdom to pursue the right path for your life.

Scripture to Meditate:

- "Therefore, humble yourselves under the mighty hand of God, that He may exalt you in due time, casting all your care upon Him, for He cares for you" (I Peter 5:7).
- "For God has not given us a spirit of fear, but of power and of love and of a sound mind" (2 Timothy 1:7).
- "Assuredly, I say to you, whoever says to this mountain, 'Be removed and be cast into the sea,' and does not doubt in his heart, but believes that those things he says will be done, he will have whatever he says. Therefore, I say to you, whatever things you ask when you pray, believe that you receive them, and you will have them" (Mark 11:23 – 24).

Write a prayer of faith for what you need today.

_____

_____

18

How Does Your
Garden Grow?

Read Mark 4:1 – 9. Jesus is talking about the heart preparedness of people to receive the seed of the word of God. In some, the seed is not given much thought, and Satan comes immediately and takes away what was sown. Other seed fell on stony soil; I believe this could be a heart that is littered with rocks of legalism (Old Testament law-based religion). The seed didn't have much soil in which to grow, so, although it germinated quickly, the roots had no depth because of the rocks underneath. Consequently, it withered away when the heat of opposition came. Some seed fell on thorny soil, where the heart is distracted by the cares of this world, and desires for other things crowd out God's word so the seed bears no fruit. Then there are those who gladly hear the Word, take it to heart, and produce varying percentages of increase.

We plant the seed of the Word as we consistently read and apply that word to our life. "Those who plant in tears will harvest with shouts of joy. They weep as they go to plant their seed, but they sing as they return with the harvest" (Psalm 126:5 – 6, NLT). When a situation needs changed, we believers have the privilege (and responsibility) to sow God's word into that situation. We do that as we declare God's promises, in faith, over the situation.

In Genesis 1:2 – 3 we read that "The earth was without form, and void, and darkness was on the face of the deep. And the Spirit of God was hovering over the face of the waters. Then God said, 'Let there be light, and there was light.'" I picture the Spirit of God hovering over a situation, just waiting for the release of God's word (His promise) to be spoken, so He can bring about what is needed. Bill Johnson, Bible teacher and pastor of Bethel church in Redding, California, commented, "Without God, we can't; without us, He won't." He needs us to be His voice in the earth to agree with what He promised.

In Mark 11:22 – 23 Jesus said, "Have faith in God. For assuredly, I say to you, whoever says to this mountain, 'Be removed and be cast into the sea,' and does not doubt in his heart, but believes that those things he says will be done, he will have whatever he says."

To be sure, we may plant (speak in faith) the seeds of God's word with tears, but if we don't uproot the seed by speaking contrary to what God says, we will eventually reap the harvest with joy! All His promises are "Yes" and "Amen" in Jesus! Hallelujah!

Declare: I guard the soil of my heart and take charge of my garden. I refuse to let the cares of life crowd out the word of God. I allow the Holy Spirit to prepare my heart to receive God's goodness and truth, so my soil produces a good crop of righteousness, peace, and joy!

What promise(s) from God are you sowing into your life today?

_____

_____

19

God is Good; the Devil is Bad

"Every good gift and every perfect gift is from above, and comes down from the Father of lights, with whom there is no variation or shadow of turning" (James 1:17). God is so very good; He can't be any other way. Some have erroneously attributed sickness, disease, tragedy, storms, trouble and death, to God, saying that He must have some purpose for "allowing" these things in the life of a Christian.

No, my friend. People somehow forget there is a thief, the devil, who comes only to steal, kill, and destroy. But Jesus, God's Son, came to earth that we may have life, and have it more abundantly (See John 10:10). Scripture also tells us that the last enemy to be destroyed is death (I Corinthians 15:26). Sickness, tragedy, trouble, and death is not from God!

In his book, *God is Good*, Bill Johnson makes the point that Jesus, during His time on earth, did nothing as the Son of God, but chose to live with the restrictions of a man (see Philippians 2:7). Bill writes, "One of the most common phrases used is, 'God is in control.' It is true that He is the Sovereign God. He reigns over all, and everything belongs to Him. He is all-knowing and all-powerful. . . but does that make Him responsible for Hitler? Is brain cancer His idea? If He is in control, then we must credit Him with disease, earthquakes, hurricanes, and all the other calamities in life. While we oversee our own homes, not everything that happens under our roof is necessarily our idea or approved by us." So often Christians say God has a reason for "allowing" tragedies, that He "has a reason." Bill continues, "That is lazy theology that somehow releases us from responsibility by shifting the blame to a God who put us in charge over the works of His hands."

Pastor and teacher Gregory Dickow said, "If you believe that everything that happens in life was pre-destined by God, then you will lower your defenses against the devil. And Satan would love for you to just accept whatever comes in life as God's will. This requires no faith, no battle, and leads to no victory."

We have been given authority by Jesus in Luke 10:19: "Behold, I give you the authority to trample on serpents and scorpions, and over all the power of the enemy, and nothing shall by any means hurt you." We are to rule in the earth and subdue it. Keep the snake out. Jesus said Satan comes only to steal, kill, and destroy, but He came that we might have life, and have it in abundance (John 10:10). We have been made "kings and priests to His God and Father; to Him be the glory and dominion forever and ever" (Revelation 1:6). We are co-laborers with God our Father (I Corinthians 3:9).

God spoke the creation into existence in Genesis chapter one, and we are to be imitators of God, to speak things into existence by His faith. Even regarding receiving our own salvation, Romans 10:8 – 10 declares, "But what does it say? 'The word is near you, in your mouth and in your heart' (that is, the word of faith which we preach): that if you confess with your mouth the Lord Jesus and believe in your heart that God has raised Him from the dead, you will be saved. For with the heart one believes unto righteousness, and with the mouth confession is made unto salvation."

Jesus says, "Have faith in God. For assuredly, I say to you, whoever says to this mountain, "Be removed and be cast into the sea," and does not doubt in his heart, but believes that those things he says will be done, he will have whatever he says" (Mark 11:23). The words of our

ELAINE BEACHY

mouth are powerful when they come from the heart. We must speak
things that agree with God's Word—not carnal things. God's promises
are words of life—never death.

Bill Johnson makes the statement, "I will not sacrifice my knowledge
of the goodness of God on the altar of human reasoning so that I can
have an explanation for why a tragedy happened. But one thing is for
sure: He is good—and He is always better than we think."

Scripture to Meditate:

- "And we desire that each one of you show the same diligence to
  the full assurance of hope until the end, that you do not become
  sluggish, but imitate those who through faith and patience
  inherit the promises" (Hebrews 6:11 – 12).
- "Death and life are in the power of the tongue, and those who
  love it will eat its fruit" (Proverbs 18:21).

Write your declaration of faith for God's intervention in a situation
you're facing today.

_____

_____

20

A Weapon Called Joy

One evening when my Amish Grandma Ollie had dinner guests, she opened the refrigerator door to pull out the dessert pie; it slipped from her hands and landed upside-down on the floor! My mom witnessed the event and said Ollie just started to sing, cleaned up the whole mess, and didn't utter one word of anger or complaint. Amazing!

I believe this statement is so true: "If the devil can't steal your joy, he can't keep your goods!" We know the devil wants to steal our health, finances, peace, joy, love, etc. He especially wants to steal our joy, because joy releases the power of hope in us. He wants to make us give up believing God's promises and put evil thoughts into our minds. We can have joy when we know the character of God, that He's always faithful to His promises, no matter what our outward circumstances might be shouting at us. The devil's devious plan is to make us feel hopeless, so we will lose faith in God.

For the Christian, joy is a fruit of the Holy Spirit in us. Galatians 5:22 – 23 tells us, "But the fruit of the Spirit is love, joy, peace, longsuffering, kindness, goodness, faithfulness, gentleness, self-control. Against such there is no law." And Isaiah 12:3 says, "Therefore with joy you will draw water from the wells of salvation," anytime we need it. Having joy is a decision, not necessarily a feeling such as happiness, which is based on good outward circumstances. Joy is rooted in knowing God's character, being steadfast, immovable, and choosing to declare God's word and stand on it, regardless of how we feel.

There's something powerful that happens in the spirit realm when we choose to sing instead of to complain, to talk to ourselves in psalms, hymns, and spiritual songs instead of harboring resentment or bitterness, and lift holy hands in worship and faith toward God. I have also clapped my hands in song, in defiance of the way I felt physically. Praise defeats the enemy of our soul and strengthens us in the Lord!

Psalm 91:4 says, "He shall cover you with His feathers, and under His wings you shall take refuge; His truth shall be your shield and buckler." I picture God's feathers covering me, so that attacks of the devil roll off me like water off a duck's back. They don't penetrate. Hallelujah!

Acting on the word of God, and not just reading or hearing it, is necessary for victory in our lives. We can be joyful and shout for joy, even when we don't yet see the answer to our prayers. I believe praise and joy are spiritual weapons against our enemy, the devil, who only comes to steal, kill, and destroy.

Scripture to Meditate:

- "But let those rejoice who put their trust in You; let them ever shout for joy, because You defend them; let those also who love Your name be joyful in You. For You, O Lord, will bless the righteous; with favor You will surround him as with a shield."
- "A merry heart does good like a medicine, but a broken spirit dries the bones" Proverbs 17:22).
- "Then he said to them, 'Go your way, eat the fat, drink the sweet, and send portions to those for whom nothing is prepared.

For this day is holy to our Lord. Do not sorrow, for the joy of the Lord is your strength'" (Nehemiah 8:10).

Write out a declaration of joy over a difficult situation.

_____

_____

21

What Do You Think?

One of my favorite faith-building and comforting scriptures in the Bible is Psalm ninety-one. I have turned to it countless times for comfort, reassurance, to build my faith, and find victory in painful situations. I made a Word document of that scripture, laminated it, stuck a little magnet at the top in back, and put it on my refrigerator where I can see it daily.

One Sunday someone said some very hurtful things to me, and I was struggling to have a right frame of mind. I felt unusually deeply wounded to the point of an ache in my chest. As my husband and I ate lunch, I discussed the pain with him, and inwardly asked the Holy Spirit to help me overcome this emotional pain. I suddenly thought of my laminated Psalm ninety-one document, and verses four and five came to memory: "He shall cover you with His feathers, and under His wings you shall take refuge; His truth shall be your shield and buckler. You shall not be afraid of the terror by night, nor of the arrow that flies by day. . ." That last phrase about arrows stood out to me.

God showed me that those hurtful words were like flaming arrows sent by the devil to wound me. As that scripture went into my heart, the arrows came out, and I was totally healed and set free from the hurt. I don't even remember who it was or what was said; God has so thoroughly set me free from it! That's the power of God's word!

Thank God, we have the power to choose our thoughts and speak God's promises! Had I chosen to dwell on the hurt I'd experienced instead of turning to God for comfort, I would have been miserable for a long time, and Satan could have used it to bring division and alienation toward that person.

Studies show that thoughts and words (positive or negative) affect one's immune system and general health. Proverbs 4:22 states that God's words "are life and health to those who find them, and health to all their flesh." Isn't that awesome? When sickness attacks, we need to stand on scriptures about health and healing, such as First Peter 2:24 that tells us by Jesus' stripes we were healed.

We can bring a thought into captivity, arrest it, put it into jail, and give it the death sentence, in Jesus' name. We can replace those wrong thoughts with godly ones. The devil cannot keep us in the wrong frame of mind. Someone once said, "You can't stop the birds from flying over your head, but you can stop them from building nests in your hair."

Scripture to Meditate:

- "Let the words of my mouth and the meditation of my heart be acceptable in Your sight, O Lord, my strength and my Redeemer" (Psalm 19:4).
- "For the weapons of our warfare are not carnal, but mighty in God for pulling down strongholds, casting down arguments and every high thing that exalts itself against the knowledge of God, bringing every thought into captivity to the obedience of Christ" (2 Corinthians 10:4 – 5).
- "God has not given us a spirit of fear, but of power, and of love, and of a sound mind" (2 Timothy 1:7).
- "Finally, brethren, whatever things are true, whatever things are noble, whatever things are just, whatever things are pure, whatever things are lovely, whatever things are of good report,

if there is any virtue and if there is anything praiseworthy –
meditate on these things" (Philippians 4:8).

Where do you want to change your thinking?

_____

_____

22

Love Your Enemies

Jesus said in Matthew 5:44 – 4 8, "But I say to you, 'love your enemies, bless those who curse you, do good to those who hate you, and pray for those who spitefully use you and persecute you, that you may be sons of your Father in heaven; for He makes His sun rise on the evil and on the good, and sends rain on the just and the unjust. For if you love those who love you, what reward have you? Do not even the tax collectors do the same? And if you greet your brethren only, what do you do more than others? Do not even the tax collectors do so? Therefore, you shall be perfect, just as your Father in heaven is perfect."

When someone cuts us off in traffic, or takes that ideal parking space we wanted, or gets the job promotion we expected, what do we feel in our heart? Anger? Resentment? Bitterness? And in this politically-charged climate, what about those with whom we disagree? I know families suffer division over politics and spiritual beliefs, and it can feel like those who disagree with us are the enemy. But Jesus calls us to love one another regardless of our differences. We are to be friendly, respectful, kind, helpful, and give hugs and words of encouragement when they face life's challenges. We are to pray for one another and ask God's best for them, not engage in angry arguments. We are to refuse to hold grudges and bless them instead.

Finally, let's take to heart Romans 12:17 – 21 (Amplified Bible): "Repay no one evil for evil, but take thought for what is honest and proper and noble [aiming to be above reproach] in the sight of everyone. If possible, as far as it depends on you, live at peace with everyone. Beloved, never avenge yourselves, but leave the way open for [God's] wrath; for it is written, 'Vengeance is Mine, I will repay (requite),' says the Lord. But if your enemy is hungry, feed him; if he is thirsty, give him drink; for by so doing you will heap burning coals upon his head. Do not let yourself be overcome by evil but overcome (master) evil with good."

Scripture to Meditate:

- "So then, my beloved brethren, let every man be swift to hear, slow to speak, slow to wrath; for the wrath of man does not produce the righteousness of God" (James 1:19 – 20).
- "For where envy and self-seeking exist, confusion and every evil thing is there" (James 3:16).
- "And just as you want men to do to you, you also do them likewise" (Luke 6:31).

Declare: I choose to love my enemies. I pray for _____ to be blessed by God's love.

_____

_____

23

Pray for Your Children

Besides Television Street and Computer Avenue being dangerous places for children to play, drugs, alcohol, and promiscuous behavior threaten their spiritual health and safety if they associate with the wrong peers. Schools with liberal philosophies on sex education, evolution, and moral relativism threaten to erode godly values parents may have tried to instill at home. What's a parent to do?

Some parents make financial sacrifices and enroll their children in expensive private or Christian schools to protect them from wrong influences. But, human nature being what it is without Jesus, there is no guarantee that even in Christian schools, safety from every threat will be found.

You install television and computer filters to help protect your children. You are careful to watch over your child's friendships. If you're a Christian parent, I know you care deeply that your child receives salvation by faith in Jesus Christ. You've cultivated a godly atmosphere of love in your home and taught the word of God to them. But still you struggle with worry and fears because of unprecedented challenges your children face today.

As children spread their wings and "fly from the nest," many parents worry whether they have done enough to disciple their children in the ways of the Lord. They wonder, what if they walk away from Jesus? What if they marry the wrong person? What if they choose the wrong career? What if they adopt New Age teaching, get sucked into the occult or witchcraft?

I have hope and good news for you: declare the word of God over your children! "The word of God is living and powerful, and sharper than any two-edged sword" (Hebrews 4:12). Stop praying in fear. Stop seeing your child in the enemy's hands! Declare the word of the Lord with the power and authority Jesus gave you! You will find hope and faith arise in your heart when you do. It gives God a framework of faith in which to work on their behalf. Claim God's promises about your children, and stand on them in persistent faith, no matter how circumstances look. Speak life! Choose words based on what God says about your children and declare them prayerfully, with faith in God. Don't say things like:

- My kids are a pain in the neck.
- Suzie will never change.
- Satan has my kids.
- Johnny is no good.

Do you want those words to bear fruit? I don't think so. You should be aware that parents who repeatedly say or think such things give the devil legal license and an inroad into their children's lives. Proverbs 18:20 says that the power of life and death are in the power of the tongue. Continually declare such things as:

- My children are a blessing.
- God is doing a good work in Suzie's life.
- My children are taught of the Lord.
- God will fulfill His plan in Johnny's life.
- I'm blessed to be entrusted with raising children for the Lord.

One of my favorite scriptures to pray over my children is Isaiah 54:13: "All your children shall be taught by the Lord, and great shall be the peace of your children." Another one is, "I will pour out My Spirit on all flesh; your sons and daughters shall prophesy, your young men shall see visions" (Acts 2:17). And Proverbs 22:6 says, "Train a child in the way he should go, and when he is old he will not depart from it." Put your children's names in the Scripture verses and say them back to God. Believe that God is at work as you bless your children with these words.

"For as the rain comes down, and the snow from heaven, and do not return there, but water the earth, and make it bring forth and bud, that it may give seed to the sower and bread to the eater, so shall My word be that goes forth from My mouth; it shall not return to Me void, but it shall accomplish what I please, and it shall prosper in the thing for which I sent it" (Isaiah 55:10 – 11). God gave us His promises to speak in the earth that He may establish them. It's the Genesis law of sowing and reaping. Your words are spiritual seeds; choose them carefully. The crop you raise will be your own.

Remember that Proverbs 18:21 says, "The tongue has the power of life and death, and those who love it will eat its fruit." The Lord has given us very great and precious promises that are realized when we speak our faith in His word, and with persistent patience, wait on the Lord to bring about the fulfillment. Like a farmer who plants his crops in the earth, and waits for the harvest, so we sow into the spiritual realm with the words of our mouth. What kind of harvest do you want? It's important to say what God says about you, your family, and your circumstances.

For more on speaking God's word over your children, I recommend Mike Shreve's book, *65 Promises from God for Your Child—Powerful Prayers for Supernatural Results.*

Declare: My children are faithful disciples of the Lord Jesus!

Write down a promise about your child. Perhaps you want to also write it on an index card and post it where you can see it regularly.

_____

_____

24

Pass the Salt, Please

"You are the salt of the earth, but if the salt loses its flavor, how shall it be seasoned? It is then good for nothing but to be thrown out and trampled underfoot by men. You are the light of the world. A city that is set on a hill cannot be hidden. Nor do they light a lamp and put it under a bushel, but on a lampstand, and it gives light to all who are in the house. Let your light so shine before men, that they may see your good works and glorify your Father in heaven" (Matthew 5:13 – 16).

Salt is a preservative, particularly of meat, because it dries up the moisture in food, so bacteria can't multiply. Jesus said we believers are the salt of the earth—preservers of society by influencing those around us. But if "salty believers" lose their salt, how shall it (the world) be seasoned? If believers become influenced by the world, rather than the other way around, their testimony is good for nothing, and the world discounts and tramples them.

We often say that the twinkling lights of Christmas represent Jesus as the light of the world. But Jesus said we believers are also the light of the world! What a privilege! I picture believers as a lighthouse, standing straight and tall, shining our beacon of light out across the dark waters of society to help draw people to Jesus their Savior—the only One who can save them from destruction.

Let's keep our lights shining, and not be like those Jesus described in John 3:19 – 21, ". . .Men loved darkness rather than light, because their deeds were evil. For everyone practicing evil hates the light and does not come to the light, lest his deeds should be exposed. But he who does the truth comes to the light, that his deeds may be clearly seen, that they have been done in God."

Second Corinthians 4:3 – 4 states, "But even if our gospel is veiled, it is veiled to those who are perishing, whose minds the god of this world has blinded, who do not believe, lest the light of the glory of Christ, who is the image of God, should shine on them." When we pray for someone who is in darkness, we can command the blinders to be removed, pray that God would shine the light of the gospel into their hearts, and send people across their path to tell them of His salvation. What a privilege to co-labor with God in our sphere of influence!

We want to heed Matthew 28:18 – 20: "And Jesus came and spoke to them, saying, 'All authority has been given to Me in heaven and on earth. Go therefore and make disciples of all the nations, baptizing them in the name of the Father and of the Son and of the Holy Spirit, teaching them to observe all things that I have commanded you; and lo, I am with you always, even to the end of the age.' Amen."

Declare: I am a salty Christian, a good ambassador for the Kingdom of God!

Do you need to make any of your words match your actions?

_____

_____

25

Sunsets and Anger

"Be angry, and do not sin; do not let the sun go down on your wrath, nor give place to the devil." Did you ever wonder what exactly this passage in Ephesians 4:26 – 27 is talking about? Does it mean one can be angry until bedtime, and then we must repent of it? For years, I used to think it meant one should never go to bed angry. And while it is quite true we should never carry a grudge, I have come to see that it means "Don't let your righteous anger die out!" Don't give place to the devil by losing your righteous hatred of sin. Jesus said we are to be angry, and not sin; we are to be angry at sin, not complacent about it. It's deadly. Don't let the sun go down on your righteous anger. To fear the Lord is to hate evil (Proverbs 8:13). Would we let a cobra snake stay in our house and not deal with it? Sin is deadly, and we are not to coddle it.

James 4:4 – 8 says, "Adulterers and adulteresses! Do you not know that friendship with the world is enmity with God? Whoever therefore wants to be a friend of the world makes himself an enemy of God. Or do you think that the Scripture says in vain, 'The Spirit who dwells in us yearns jealously?' But He gives more grace. Therefore, He says, 'God resists the proud, but gives grace to the humble.' Therefore, submit to God. Resist the devil and he will flee from you. Draw near to God and He will draw near to you."

The root word of "jealously" in the above scripture means "zealous." God is zealous toward us, not passive. His love pursues us to restore fellowship with Him. Submitting to God means submitting to His Word. God corrects us through His Word—not with sickness, calamity, distress, disease, etc. Speaking of God's correction, it is written in John 15:3 that Jesus said to His disciples, "You are already clean because of the word which I have spoken to you." Aren't you glad? Let's receive His correction and have a holy hatred for sin! Amen? Amen.

Declare: I love righteousness and hate evil.

Write a prayer for yourself about righteous anger.

_____

_____

26

Soul Food

When we are born again, God writes His law on our hearts, and we grow to know what pleases or displeases Him. It's vital that we read the word of God to stimulate godly living. Second Timothy 3:16 – 17 declares, "All Scripture is given by inspiration of God, and is profitable for doctrine, for reproof, for correction, for instruction in righteousness, that the man of God may be complete, thoroughly equipped for every good work." (The word "man" is not gender specific but means "anyone.")

The book of Proverbs is filled with wonderful wisdom for daily living. Dr. Ben Carson, the world-famous brain surgeon, said he read the book of Proverbs daily as a teenager. He used to have a terrible anger problem, but God changed his heart through reading these scriptures. If you've never seen the movie of his life story, *Healing Hands,* I encourage you to see it. Raised in poverty by a single mom who couldn't read, she required them to read a certain number of books per week and give her a book report, which she pretended to read. Dr. Carson, because of his focus on reading Proverbs (which he continues to this day), went from what his fellow classmates called "the dumbest kid in the world" to a brilliant man. She limited their television viewing as well. At a time when other boys their age joined gangs and got into trouble, Mrs. Carson kept her sons occupied with reading.

Everything one does comes from deposits made in the heart. Our spiritual diet is important; one cannot feed on questionable/violent movies, books, and television programs, and not be affected negatively by them. "Above all else, guard your heart, for it is the wellspring of life. Put away perversity from your mouth; keep corrupt talk far from your lips. Let your eyes look straight ahead, fix your gaze directly before you. Make level paths for your feet and take only ways that are firm. Do not swerve to the right or the left; keep your foot from evil" (Proverbs 4:23 – 27, NIV). Proverbs 13:20 declares, "He who walks with wise men will be wise, but the companion of fools will be destroyed."

We want to feed on good things and refuse to let our minds become a garbage dump for worldly "wisdom." God's word is a lamp to our feet, and a light to our path; reading it will give us wisdom, direction, and success in life.

Declare: I feed on encouraging, positive things for my mind. I feed on the word of God!

Write down the Scripture that means the most to you right now, and why.

_____

_____

27

God Wants You Well

When I am faced with a health challenge, I immediately take the authority Jesus gave us, speak to the infirmity and command it to leave, in Jesus' name. As I Peter 5:9 instructs, resist the devil's work, steadfast in the faith. I declare Scripture promises about healing, for they are spiritual seeds of power sown into the unseen world to bring forth that which is not yet seen.

I bless myself and declare I am healed! Romans 4:17 tells us that "God calls those things which do not exist as though they did." We are to be imitators of God as dear children (Ephesians 5:1), so we too need to call forth the end from the beginning. We need to declare that the healing already provided for by Jesus shows up in our bodies. We need to declare the Scripture back to God our Father, and believe the healing, already provided by Jesus, shows up in our bodies.

"For as the rains come down from heaven, and do not return there, but water the earth, and make it bring forth and bud, that it may give seed to the sower and bread to the eater, so shall My word be that goes forth from My mouth; it shall not return to Me void, but it shall accomplish what I please, and it shall prosper in the thing for which I sent it" (Isaiah 55:10 – 11). We return God's word to Him by speaking it. And again, God says ". . . I am watching to see that my word is fulfilled" (Jeremiah 1:12, NIV).

God put his power into words; I don't understand it, but it's true. The power of God is in the seed of the Word to produce after its kind, just as seeds are in vegetation as written in Genesis 1:11: "Then God said, 'Let the earth bring forth grass, the herb that yields seed, and the fruit tree that yields fruit according to its kind, whose seed is in itself, on the earth, and it was so.' And the earth brought forth grass, the herb that yields seed according to its kind, and the tree that yields fruit, whose seed is in itself according to its kind. And God saw that it was good."

Consider the following Scripture: "Jesus answered and said to them, 'Assuredly, I say to you, if you have faith and do not doubt, you will not only do what was done to the fig tree, but also if you say to this mountain, 'Be removed and be cast into the sea,' it will be done. And whatever things you ask in prayer, believing, you will receive" (Matthew 21:21). Whatever our "mountain" situation may be, we can stand on this scripture and follow Jesus' example of cursing the fig tree. Sickness, disease, poverty, etc., must bow the knee to King Jesus and to the authority He delegated to us. Matthew 10:8 says, "Heal the sick, cleanse the lepers, raise the dead, cast out demons. Freely you have received, freely give."

And please don't stumble over the religious interpretation of "Paul's thorn in the flesh" that is so often used to say that it is not always God's will to heal. In studying chapters eleven and twelve of Second Corinthians in context, and by revelation of the Spirit, I have come to see that Paul's thorn clearly means people who withstood him and his message. He was beaten, stoned, shipwrecked, harassed, in danger, etc., many times. (I encourage you to read both of those chapters). I can well imagine Paul despaired of this terrible treatment. I would too!

In interpreting Scripture, it's important to use the law of first mention. The term, "thorn in the flesh," was first used in Numbers 33:55 where God told the Israelites if they didn't drive out those living in the lands they conquered, the heathen nations would become "irritants in your eyes and thorns in your sides, and they will harass you in the land where you dwell." People who harassed Paul who were "thorns in his side." God never said He'd take people out of our way—He wants them all to repent and be saved. And God gave him grace to endure the opposition that came, just as Jesus did in His earthly ministry.

No matter how long it takes, God says we will reap if we don't give up (Galatians 6:9). And, "Through faith and patience, we inherit the promises" (Hebrews 6:12). Be encouraged today to stand firm for your healing, or for that painful situation to be turned around from wrong to right.

Scripture to Meditate:

- "'For I will restore health to you and heal you of your wounds,' says the Lord" (Jeremiah 30:17).
- "But He was wounded for our transgressions. He was bruised for our iniquities; the chastisement for our peace was upon Him, and by His stripes we are healed" (Isaiah 53:5).
- "Beloved, I pray that you may prosper in all things and be in health, just as your soul prospers" (3 John 1:2).
- "Jesus went about . . . preaching the gospel of the kingdom and healing all kinds of sickness and all kinds of disease among the people" (Matthew 4:23).
- "God anointed Jesus of Nazareth with the Holy Spirit and with power, who went about doing good and healing all who were oppressed by the devil, for God was with Him" (Acts 10:38).
- "Behold, I give you the authority to trample on serpents and scorpions, and over all the power of the enemy, and nothing shall by any means hurt you" (Luke 10:19).
- "Who Himself bore our sins in His own body on the tree, that we, having died to sins, might live for righteousness—by whose stripes you were healed" (I Peter 2:24).

If you need healing, write out your declaration of faith in God's promises.

_____

_____

28

The Christmas Bonus

The year 1987 was one of great change and adjustment for our family, as we left Pennsylvania and moved to Virginia with our three children. Although my parents, brothers and their families all lived in the same area of Virginia, I felt the great loss of friendships and certain social positions I'd enjoyed in Pennsylvania. I had been president of our local chapter of Women's Aglow, had been heavily involved in our church at Indian Lake Christian Center, as well as a home Bible study. Here in Virginia, I was a "nobody." The neighbors and roads were new, traffic was heavier and faster, we had to find a new church and make new friends. We felt led to go to a different church than my parents and brothers attended, so we didn't see them on a regular basis. Everyone seemed involved in their own face-paced lifestyle and circle of friends.

Now, in a few days, we'd be celebrating our second Christmas in Virginia. Smiling faces and excited chatter greeted me as our family of five gathered for dinner on that December evening years ago. Our oldest son told of a bonus check he'd received from his boss, and our daughter said she also received one from her employer. My husband got a nice Christmas bonus as well.

I told each one I was glad for them, but suddenly the monster of self-pity reared its ugly head and hissed in my ear: "Where is your bonus? Everyone except you is doing something worthwhile and getting rewarded for it." My throat tightened, and I turned away so they wouldn't see my tears. What was the matter with me?

The family ate in fifteen minutes what had taken me hours to prepare. Afterwards, my teenage boys headed to their bedrooms downstairs and my daughter to hers down the hall from the kitchen. My husband went to the living room to watch TV, and I was left alone, staring at a messy table and even more kitchen duty. Where was my free time? Resentment squeezed hard, sending streams of tears down my cheeks. I felt cheated, unappreciated, taken for granted, and worthless. The emotional pain in my chest was palpable as the monster stabbed me.

Feeling quite sorry for myself, I shuffled around the table, stacked plates and silverware, and plodded to the kitchen. I looked out the kitchen window into the inky black of night, set the plates in the sink, then headed back to the dining room for another load of dirty dishes. I gave my husband a furtive glance to see if he'd volunteer to help. Nope, he was enjoying his television program. Suddenly, I remembered the words of Bible teacher Joyce Meyer: "You can either be pitiful or powerful, but you can't be both."

I straightened my shoulders and decided the monster had played his last hand. I dismissed him with a stiff rebuke, and he fled in terror at the name of Jesus. The Holy Spirit helped me realize that Jesus will reward me for ministering to my family. Jesus was my Christmas bonus, and I was honored to serve Him by caring for my loved ones. What could be better than that?

Scripture to Meditate:

- "Rejoice with those who rejoice, and weep with those who weep" (Romans 12:15).
- "Love suffers long and is kind; love does not envy. . ." (I Corinthians 13:4).

- "A sound heart is life to the body, but envy is rottenness to the bones" (Proverbs 14:30).
- "Wrath is cruel and anger a torrent, but who is able to stand before jealousy?" (Proverbs 27:4)

Declare: I refuse to be pitiful; I am not a victim! I am strong in the Lord, and in the power of His might!

Where have you had victory over self-pity and resentment?

_____

_____

29

The Battle for the Mind

According to Dr. Caroline Leaf, famous cognitive neuroscientist, 75% of all illness is a direct result of our thoughts. The average person has about 30,000 thoughts per day! Wow, that's a lot of thinking! Dr. Leaf has worked in brain science since 1985, and she says scientific principles are supported by Scripture and vice-versa. In her book, *Who Switched Off My Brain,* she shows how our thoughts appear in scientific images as tiny trees called dendrites. When a person is impacted by toxic thoughts, the "trees" turn black and grow little thorns. Amazing!

The battle for the mind began in the Garden of Eden, when Satan challenged Eve to eat of the forbidden tree. The devil used half-truths and twisted what God had said. He lied to her, and she chose to believe him. Her thoughts led to an action, which affected her husband and the whole human race. (I think Adam deserves the blame too, because he didn't try to stop her. Scripture says he was with her at the time). And we know the rest of the story, how all of mankind was infected by sin.

The root of our destiny (what we become) is our thoughts. Proverbs 23:7 tells us "For as he thinks in his heart, so is he." Thoughts determine decisions; decisions determine actions; actions determine habits; habits determine character, and character determines destiny.

Philippians 4:6 – 7 says, "Be anxious for nothing, but in everything by prayer and supplication, with thanksgiving, let your requests be made known to God; and the peace of God, which surpasses all understanding, will guard your hearts and minds through Christ Jesus." And in Philippians 4:8, the Lord instructs us to think about these things:

- Whatever is true: Lies and gossip have destroyed more than one person's reputation.
- Whatever is noble: Honor those who live a life of godly behavior.
- Whatever is right: Base all beliefs on God's Word and relationship with Him.
- Whatever is pure: Don't mix law and grace; be established in pure righteousness.
- Whatever is lovely: Enjoy the beauty of God's creation and the beauty of His people.
- Whatever is of good report: Think and talk about the good things people do.
- Whatever is virtuous: Choose godly friends, good books, modest dress and behavior.
- Whatever is praiseworthy: Think about all the goodness of the Lord, who is worthy of all praise.

We need to control and direct our thoughts, because our mind plays an important part for victory in life.

Scripture to Meditate:

- "I will meditate on Your precepts and contemplate Your ways. I will delight myself in Your statutes; I will not forget Your word" (Psalm 119:15 – 16).
- "Blessed is the man who walks not in the counsel of the ungodly, nor stands in the path of sinners, nor sits in the seat of the

scornful; but his delight is in the law of the Lord, and in His law, he meditates day and night" (Psalm 1:1 – 2).

- "My son, give attention to my words; incline your ear to my sayings. Do not let them depart from your eyes; keep them in the midst of your heart; for they are life to those who find them, and health to all their flesh. Keep your heart with all diligence, for out of it spring the issues of life" (Proverbs 4:20 – 23).

What challenges do you face in obeying God's command to think on good things?

_____

_____

Love

Everyone needs love and friendship. Who can forget the cute "puppy love" valentines you received in elementary school? Or the homemade valentines you made with crayons, markers, water colors, construction paper, and bits of ribbon or lace? Or the little multi-colored candy hearts with the words, "Be Mine," "Hug Me," "Real Love," etc.? Maybe you purchased your valentines to share with classmates or mailed them to friends.

As I thought about love, I decided to write a poem based on First Corinthians thirteen in the Bible.

What is love?

Love is the glue
That keeps friendship from crumbling.
Love is the arm
That keeps you from stumbling.

Love is the look
That says, "It's okay,"
When you've blown it so badly
Or gone your own way.

Love is the joy
When truth wins the day,
Iniquities pardoned—
Not put on display.

Love is no joke;
It's sincere and kind,
Not rude or proud,
But peace for the mind.

Yes, love never fails,
And our God is love.
Our cues come from Him
On the wings of a Dove.

God sent you a Valentine: Jesus! God's valentine reads, "Will you be Mine? Even before you were born, I loved you so much that I sent My Son into your world to die for your sins to restore your and My relationship. Please be My valentine."

Dear reader, if you accept God's valentine offer, pray this prayer: "Jesus, I accept Your forgiveness of my sins. I declare that You are my Lord, and I believe in my heart that God raised You from the dead. I thank You for Your promise that anyone who calls on Your name will be saved. Thank You for loving me; thank you for saving me, Jesus." (From Romans 10:9 – 13).

Who has God put on your heart to love more perfectly?

_____

_____

HAPPY VALENTINE'S DAY!

31

Be Filled with the Holy Spirit

As a newlywed, I was nervous and curious when Dave and I went with a couple who invited us to attend a meeting of the Full Gospel Businessmen's Fellowship in Somerset, Pennsylvania. As I sat and listened to testimonies of those who had been baptized in the Holy Spirit with the evidence of speaking in tongues, I became highly offended. My thought was, "I'm as good a Christian as they are; I don't need this stuff." As we left the meeting, I walked past a table of free books and, merely on impulse, picked up one titled *Aglow with the Spirit* by Dr. Robert Frost. My reasoning? This book was written by an educated person; he won't be weird. Little did I know how that book would change my life.

The next day when Dave went to work, I took the book out of hiding and sat down on the couch in our mobile home to read it. As I read, the Spirit of God opened my eyes to the truth of Scripture, and about halfway through the book, my pride crumbled, and I wept as I knelt beside the couch and asked Jesus to baptize me in the Holy Spirit. The desire to pray in an unknown language rose up in me, and in timid faith I obeyed that desire. The more I prayed in that unintelligible language, the bolder and more refreshed I felt. Then I heard Dave's car in the driveway, and I quickly jumped up and hid the book again.

After dinner, as I washed the dishes, a sudden fearful thought came over me: "You have really sinned now! Praying in tongues is of the devil!" In panic, with no one to turn to for help, I secluded myself in our bedroom and turned to the Lord. I felt led to pray in tongues with all my might. And in that moment, I knew the devil had lied to me, that the Holy Spirit was a real friend, and to be trusted. Eventually, my husband, my parents, and others in our church also received the baptism of the Holy Spirit with the evidence of speaking in tongues, as I shared my book with them.

Word got around about our experience, and we paid a price. The owners of the land we rented as a site for our mobile home came to the house one evening and told us we had to get off their property, citing they had "plans" for it. (Amazing how being filled with the Spirit lets one know when someone is lying.) We knew by the Spirit of God that we were being evicted because, according to their beliefs, we were "of the devil." But that's okay; it is better to obey God than man. I'd do it all over again!

Questions hesitant Christians ask about speaking in tongues:

- Didn't I receive the Holy Spirit when I became born again? The answer is "Yes." (See Romans 8:9.) When we become baptized with the Holy Spirit, He is not only in us, but flows out of us.
- Do I have to speak in tongues?" The answer is, "No, you don't have to—you are privileged to!" Perhaps an honest question to ask is, "Why wouldn't I want to?"
- Are tongues always the initial evidence of being baptized in the Holy Spirit? Acts 2:4 says, "And they were all filled with the Holy Spirit and began to speak with other tongues, as the Spirit gave them utterance."
- Why should I receive the baptism of the Holy Spirit? We are commanded to do so. (See Ephesians 5:19 – 20, Acts 1:4 – 5, John 7:38 and I Corinthians 14:1).
- What are the benefits of praying in tongues? Jude verse 20 tells us that: 1.) It builds our faith, 2.) Romans 8:26 says the Holy

Spirit helps us in our praying, and 3.) It's part of our spiritual armor (see Ephesians 6:18).

- Isn't there danger of receiving an evil spirit if I pray in tongues? No. Jesus said in Luke 11:9 – 13), "If you then, being evil, know how to give good gifts to your children, how much more will your heavenly Father give the Holy Spirit to those who ask Him!"

Why pray in tongues? Jesus commanded His disciples to wait in the upper room after His resurrection (Acts 1:8), and not begin any ministry until the Holy Spirit came upon them. They all spoke in tongues (Acts 2:4). Mary, the mother of Jesus, was also there in the upper room with the disciples and spoke in tongues as well (see Acts 1:13 – 14).

Why pray in tongues? We need victory over sin; we need divine order in our lives, and power to minister to others! We need boldness to use our authority given us by Jesus. We need to hear from God in life's situations. Jesus operated and ministered in the power of the Spirit just as He expects us to do. Read John 14:12 – 14 and Acts 2:38.

It's often difficult to yield to the Holy Spirit and begin speaking in tongues because it sounds foreign. The mind says it's childish, silly, or even demeaning; I have found it deals with our intellectual pride. That's exactly what God wants: humility. It takes faith and humility to yield our tongues to God. He has His own reasons why the Kingdom operates the way it does. I don't need to figure everything out.

The Holy Spirit is never dull, but alive, moving, and exciting. We need never be afraid of Him, for He is God's Spirit! Praying in tongues is praying the perfect will of God and praising Him with excellence. And His will is only good: all His promises are "Yes" and "Amen" in Jesus! He is always for you! Praying in tongues is a powerful spiritual weapon!

What obstacles did (or do) you face in receiving the baptism of the Holy Spirit?

_____

_____

32

Quiet, Please

Yapping dogs of discouragement and weariness nipped at my heels. Unwelcome tears stole to the corners of my eyes as I entered my quiet space and shut both doors. The sound of the dogs seemed farther away as I sat on the sofa with Bible, journal, and pen at hand. I swallowed the lump in my throat and took a deep breath. My lips quivered as I struggled to find proper prayer words, but I gave up and decided quietness was better. I thought of my Lover and closed my eyes.

Aware of His presence, I imagined a wrought iron fence that surrounded a garden, which I entered through a diagonal corner gate. Before me in the center of the garden was a beautiful, white, three-tiered water fountain. Tall geysers of crystal clear, sparkling water rocketed upward, and then fell, cascading, into its base below. Immediately, I thought, "The Water of Life, springing up to salvation."

As I looked down, a circular bed of smiling, purple-faced yellow pansies decorated the base of the fountain, and I began to weep. My Amish paternal grandmother's nickname was "Pansy," and as I cried, I thanked my heavenly Father for her years of love and faithful prayer for me. To my left I noticed a bird house atop a pole, while a small bird perched on the lower lip of the fountain to take a drink.

Enjoying the melody of the fountain, I walked past the birdhouse to a canopy swing on the soft green grass and invited my Lover to join me. We sat in peaceful silence for a while before I noticed a lidded brown box close to the fountain. I turned to Him. A bit timid, I gathered my courage and asked, "What's in the box?" Immediately I knew it contained my disappointments and weariness, and I began to weep. I spoke in a whisper, "I give You all my weariness, all my disappointments; please refresh every part of me."

He sat beside me in companionable silence, never demanding anything. My heart lifted, and I felt deeply loved, understood, warmed, and comforted. Then my day called, and the interruption annoyed me. I looked at Him and said, "I have to go."

The next day I went back to the garden with eagerness, and again invited my Lover to join me. A golden shaft of sunlight streamed onto the green grass as we sat together on the swing. Again, the box by the fountain caught my attention. My Lover looked at me and suggested, "Let's open it together." He walked with me to the box, bent down and lifted the lid. My heart leapt with surprised delight when, instead of disappointments, I saw beautiful jewels and necklaces! In the bottom of the box were His love letters to me. I made a mental note of the desire that filled my heart—the desire to read His word.

Oh, how I loved Him; there was no reproach in His look—just acceptance of me and understanding of the world I live in. He reached out a hand to me, and we smiled at one another. In playful abandon I grasped both His hands as we swirled across the soft green grass.

If those dogs try to hound me again, I know where to find my garden.

Scripture to Meditate:

- "A garden enclosed is my sister, my spouse, a spring shut up, a fountain sealed" (Song of Solomon 4:12).
- "My beloved spoke, and said to me: 'Rise up, my love, my fair one, and come away. For lo, the winter is past, the rain is over and gone. The flowers appear on the earth; the time of singing

has come, and the voice of the turtledove is heard in our land. The fig tree puts forth her green figs, and the vines with the tender grapes give a good smell. Rise up, my love, my fair one, and come away" (Song of Solomon 2:10 – 13).

- "But whoever drinks of the water that I shall give him will never thirst. But the water that I shall give him will become in him a fountain of water springing up into everlasting life" (John 4:14).
- "Come to Me, all you who labor and are heavy laden, and I will give you rest. Take My yoke upon you and learn from Me, for I am gentle and lowly in heart, and you will find rest for your souls. For My yoke is easy and My burden is light" (Matthew 11:28 – 30).
- ". . . casting all your care upon Him, for He cares for you" (I Peter 5:7).

Declare: Jesus is my Friend who sticks closer than a brother

Prayer: Thank You, Jesus, for refreshing me; thank You for loving me unconditionally. I give You all my cares, because You care for me. Amen.

How is Jesus speaking to your heart?

_____

_____

The Dog Whisperer

If you've ever watched Caesar Milan's "The Dog Whisperer" on television, and his amazing way with dogs, you've seen him use the leash, certain sounds and hand signals as training techniques. He trains them to wait, be calm and submissive.

One night, several years ago after we watched an episode of his show, I woke up around 3:30 a.m. and the following teaching came to me so strongly that I got up and wrote down what the Lord downloaded to me.

ROPE = The training leash.

R – Respect for God and all authority
O – Obedience to God's word
P – Patience; learn to wait for things from God
E – Exercise our faith in God (walk in the Spirit)

Hebrews 12:1 – 12 teaches four things we are trained (or discipled) to do:

- Endure opposition from sinful men.
- Endure hardship as discipline.

- Resist sin, put off the "old man" and put on the "new man."
- Submit to the Father of our spirits and live, really live!

A dog without proper training is a very unhappy dog. He can be fearful and anxious, tear up the furniture, snap, bite, growl, and be dangerous to those around them. God doesn't want us to be like those untrained dogs. God wants us to enjoy life and have deep inner joy! He wants us to be truly free from the tyranny of sin put on us by Satan. It is for freedom that Christ has set us free through His own blood.

Our earthly fathers corrected us, and we respected them; how much more should we respect the Father of our spirits and live, Hebrews 12:9 says. We don't discipline someone else's children, because they are not ours. Even so, God disciplines only His family, not those outside it. The conviction of the Holy Spirit through the word of God is the primary way we are disciplined.

Conviction, not condemnation, is from God. The devil is the one who condemns and says we're bad. God's heart is always to bring disorder back into divine order. Some Christians teach that God disciplines us with sickness, calamity, heartache, and all kinds of trouble. That is not scriptural! God is good, and the devil is bad. Let's not confuse the two. Jesus told His disciples in John 15:3, "You are already clean because of the word which I have spoken to you." God disciplines us with His Word, and the Holy Spirit helps us obey. Changing our minds for the better (repenting) isn't always pleasant, but eventually the fruit of obedience is a happy, well-adjusted person, able to function well throughout life. (The difference in dogs before and after Caesar Milan's training is amazing, and the same can be said about people as God trains us!)

We have free will, and when we "get into hot water," so to speak, and feel the consequences of our sin, we can turn to God in repentance and ask for help. And sometimes "stuff just happens" in life, as it does with everyone, even when we haven't done anything to cause trouble or calamity. He uses the occasion or situation to teach or "disciple" and help us, but He didn't cause it. God can and will always bring good out of every situation if we trust Him!

Scripture to Meditate:

- "My son, do not despise the chastening of the Lord, nor be discouraged when you are rebuked by Him; for whom the Lord loves He chastens, and scourges every son whom He receives" (Hebrews 12:5).
- "Now no chastening seems to be joyful for the present, but painful; nevertheless, afterward it yields the peaceable fruit of righteousness to those who have been trained by it. Therefore, strengthen the hands which hang down, and the feeble knees, and make straight paths for your feet, so that what is lame may not be dislocated, but rather be healed" (Hebrews 12:11 – 13).

Where are you being trained by God?

34

Blessing Others

As I read the book *The Grace Outpouring* by Roy Godwin, my heart said a resounding, "Yes!" God taught him to bless people rather than pray against them. He talks about how he and his wife blessed the farmers, homes, and businesses in their area, and watched in amazement as prosperity increased, crime went down, and people repented and turned to the Lord.

Then I picked up a book titled *The Power of Blessing* by Kerry Kirkwood. He tells the story of a pastor who, every day, walked by the topless nightclub in his neighborhood, and cursed it by saying, "Dry up!" After all, God was on His side because He hates sin, right? But the more he cursed it week after week, the more the nightclub seemed to flourish. One day, the Lord spoke to his heart and asked him why he's cursing the people He gave His life for—the same life given to the pastor. He then realized the blindness of people's hearts were the issue—not the business. He began to bless the people inside as he walked by each day. Guess what? Within two weeks, the once-thriving nightclub had shut its doors without any notice. What a powerful truth to realize that cursing causes darkness to thrive, and blessing turns things around for righteousness sake. Wow.

Blessings can be spoken over people (whether present or absent), homes, towns, areas, regions, nations, land, businesses, livestock, schools, etc. Kerry writes, "How exactly should we bless people? What should we say? First, we ask the Holy Spirit to help us with the words to bless before we begin, so the people will receive the blessing that the Father wishes to pour out on them: his insight, not ours; his words, not ours. We want to bless the whole person, and many people find the following blessing acronym helps them be creative in blessing:

- B Body: health, protection, strength
- L Labor: work, income, security
- E Emotional: joy, peace, hope
- S Social: love, marriage, family, friends
- S Spiritual: salvation, faith, grace

"For instance, we may bless someone as follows: 'I bless you in the name of Jesus that the fullness of his peace may flood your heart and mind, sinking deeply into every part of your being and life. I bless you that your body may be strengthened and healed so you are free to walk in the joy of the Lord.' We need to be clear always that we are blessing in the name of Jesus with his authority and anointing. All power and authority reside in him, including the power and authority to bless."

I put this truth into practice, and it felt so good to bless everyone in Jesus' name: my children, my husband, my church, my pastor, our president, our government leaders, etc. Rather than gripe and complain, be fearful, or lash out in anger and outrage at difficult people, or those who live in spiritual darkness, we believers in Jesus must begin to bless them, asking that they will experience the goodness of God. We never bless wrong behavior, but we bless the person for whom Jesus died and view them with God's heart. Romans 2:4 tells us that the goodness of God will lead people to repentance.

Let's choose to speak blessing over others! Curses like, "He'll never amount to anything," or "She is a wretched example of humanity," are words the enemy of our soul uses for destruction. Sneering and abusive speech are works of darkness, and the devil is the ruler of darkness. The more we say how awful people are, the more they will stay that way. People are not the enemy—the devil is! Speak words of blessing over others (and yourself) so God can set them free! Amen!

Scripture to Meditate:

- "He who would love life and see good days, let him refrain his tongue from evil, and his lips from speaking deceit" (I Peter 3:10).
- "With the tongue we praise our God and Father, and with it we curse men, who have been made in God's likeness. Out of the same mouth come praise and cursing. My brothers, this should not be" (James 3:9 – 10, NIV).
- "And just as you want men to do to you, you also do to them likewise" (Luke 6:31).
- "Give and it will be given to you: good measure, pressed down, shaken together, and running over will be put into your bosom. For with the same measure that you use, it will be measured back to you" (Luke 6:38).

Write a blessing over a difficult someone in your life.

_____

_____

Love the Truth

My mom impressed me with this little rhyme from the time I was a young girl:

"Speak the truth!

Speak it boldly, never fear!

Speak it so that all may hear!

Speak the truth!"

Recently I came across a statement that offered people a course of study on how Jesus came to earth and "eventually became God." I did a double-take. Jesus did not become God. He is and always was God! That "becoming God" statement reminded me of a religion that teaches man can attain "God status" by becoming progressively enlightened. That's a bunch of New Age, progressive gobbledygook.

I pray the Church will not wander from the truth and adopt intellectual and high-sounding philosophies. Scripture says in Second Corinthians 11:3, "But I fear, lest somehow, as the Serpent deceived Eve by his craftiness, so your minds may be corrupted from the simplicity that is in Christ."

The truth is, a virgin named Mary conceived Jesus by the power of the Holy Spirit, who is God. "And the angel answered and said to her (Mary), 'The Holy Spirit will come upon you, and the power of the

Highest will overshadow you; therefore, also, that Holy One who is to be born will be called the Son of God" (Luke 1:33). We need to hold to the Scripture that says, "Beyond all question, the mystery of godliness is great: He appeared in a body, was vindicated by the Spirit, was seen by angels, was preached among the nations, was believed on in the world, was taken up in glory" (I Timothy 3:16, NIV).

"Don't let anyone capture you with empty philosophies and high-sounding nonsense that come from human thinking and from the spiritual powers of this world, rather than from Christ" (Colossians 2:8, NLT). Scripture also says, "In the beginning was the Word, and the Word was with God, and the Word was God. He was in the beginning with God" (John 1:1).

Jesus always was, is, and always will be God. Be wise; be alert; check everything out with Scripture. Read the Bible for yourself, but also realize no man is an island, so get godly counsel from other Christians in a good church. Don't just scoop up anything that sounds spiritual. Throughout my life, I have always prayed, "Lord, give me a love for the truth; I want the truth, no matter what it is, for it is safety and life."

First Timothy 4:1 – 3 warns us about departing from the faith. "Now the Spirit expressly says that in latter times some will depart from the faith, giving heed to deceiving spirits and doctrines of demons, speaking lies in hypocrisy, having their own conscience seared with a hot iron, forbidding to marry, and commanding to abstain from foods which God created to be received with thanksgiving by those who believe and know the truth."

We will do well to be aware of God's instruction to us in Second Timothy 3:1 – 5: "But know this, that in the last days perilous times will come: for men will be lovers of themselves, lovers of money, boasters, proud, blasphemers, disobedient to parents, unthankful, unholy, unloving, unforgiving, slanderers, without self-control, brutal, despisers of good, traitors, headstrong, haughty, lovers of pleasure rather than lovers of God, having a form of godliness but denying its power. And from such people turn away!"

My friend, may God keep you in the true faith, the gospel of Jesus Christ!

Declare: Father, I always want to have a love for the truth. Your word is truth, and I humble myself to believe and receive it.

Write your thoughts here.

_____

_____

36

Tiles and Shuttles

Over one July fourth weekend, some of our family went to the Smithsonian Air and Space Museum in Chantilly, Virginia. As I looked at the many aircraft on display, I marveled at the mind-boggling ingenuity of inventors who created such flying machines. It indeed proves the adage that what the mind can conceive, man can achieve.

In the museum, we stood under the Discovery Shuttle, and gazed up at the twenty thousand tiles that covered much of the space craft. My daughter looked at me and remarked, "You know, Mom, every one of those tiles has a number; each tile has a specific job to do. Each tile is like a puzzle piece; it's made only for a certain spot." She paused and looked at me. "It's like the body of Christ; God fits us together, too. Each member has a certain job to do that no one else can do, a certain spot to fill that no one else can fill."

The analogy was profound. I said, "You are so right, Deb; and if a tile gets damaged, it affects the performance and mission of the shuttle. It's the same with the body of Christ." I thought of the Scripture in First Corinthians 12:12 – 27 that says the body is made up of many parts, and one part can't say to the other parts, "I don't need you." There should be no division in the body, but each part should have equal concern for the others. "If one part suffers, every part suffers with it; if one part is honored, every part rejoices with it."

Ephesians 4:15 – 16 in the New International Version reads, "Instead, speaking the truth in love, we will in all things grow up into him who is the Head, that is, Christ. From him the whole body, joined and held together by every supporting ligament, grows and builds itself up in love, as each part does its work."

Read Romans 12:3-21. Especially focus on verse 10 that reads, "Be kindly affectionate to one another with brotherly love, in honor giving preference to one another." I think of the sin of gossip and how it can destroy friendships, unity and function in the body of Christ. We must not be talebearers!

Jesus said in Matthew 18:15 – 17, "Moreover if your brother sins against you, go and tell him his fault between you and him alone. If he hears you, you have gained your brother. But if he will not hear, take with you one or two more, that by the mouth of two or three witnesses every word may be established. And if he refuses to hear them, tell it to the church. But if he refuses even to hear the church, let him be to you like a heathen and a tax collector."

I refuse to listen to any television program, radio minister or any Christian criticize other ministers of the gospel. If they see a fault in another ministry, brother or sister, they need to contact them directly, and seek to keep the unity of the Spirit. I also refuse to listen to faults expressed about a brother or sister in the church. The person who criticizes needs to stop it, and go to the other person directly, as Jesus said in the above Scripture. When we hear something bad about a friend, it colors how we view them, and our relationship with them is tarnished—maybe even destroyed. Let's look out for one another, and preserve our unity, so our "tiles" are well cared for.

Scripture to meditate:

- Galatians 6:1-2: "Brethren, if a man is overtaken in any trespass, you who are spiritual restore such a one in a spirit of gentleness, considering yourself let you also be tempted. Bear one another's burdens, and so fulfill the law of Christ."

What is God speaking to your heart about preserving unity among fellow Christians?

_____

_____

37

Old and New

I was surprised that I was weeping—of all things—over a familiar passage of Scripture in Luke 2:25 – 40. The Spirit of holiness came upon me as I sat at my kitchen table, inviting revelation from God. I wept because I sensed how the Holy Spirit honored Simeon and Anna for their quiet faithfulness in serving God from a lowly position of obscurity. They were just two old people in deep devotion to God crying out for the "new" God had promised: their long-awaited Messiah.

I imagined Simeon, perhaps just an ordinary man, living in an ordinary house in Jerusalem and loving God with all his heart. As a young man, perhaps he felt insignificant about his contribution to the nation he loved. Or perhaps he felt discouraged that he wasn't talented, smart, or gifted like others. I'd like to think he decided not to compare himself to those, and instead tucked himself in with God, and devoted his life to minister to God and await the coming Savior of his nation.

As with most Jews of that time, it's likely he was distressed by the oppression of Israel by the Romans, and by the spiritual state of his people—a corrupted culture influenced by Roman way of life and thought. Simeon chose to be a just and devout man, loving the Lord his God with all his mind, soul, and strength.

The Scripture passage says Anna was an old prophetess; I think it likely she was about one hundred and ten years old. Consider: she had been a widow for eighty-seven years, after being married seven years, which covers ninety-four years. It's probable she got married as a young girl around age sixteen (if not younger), which, added to the ninety-four, would make her one hundred and ten years old. Did she have family who could have cared for her? I don't know. I can imagine Anna as a young widow at the age of twenty-three, wondering what to do with the rest of her life that stretched before her like an empty road that disappeared into a distant mist. A road stripped of dreams she once held dear to her heart.

Like Simeon, Anna chose to devote herself to be part of God's answer for Israel by praying and fasting for her nation and the spiritual condition of her people. She prophesied God's words from heaven. Because of their faithful, whole-hearted devotion to God, Simeon, an old man, and Anna, an old woman, got to be in on the "new" God was doing.

History records other stories of the "old" helping birth the "new" that God wanted to do. The great Hebrides Scottish revival, said to have been the greatest revival of all time, was birthed shortly after World War Two because two elderly women, Peggy Smith, age eighty-4our, and Christine Smith, eighty-two, got together and constantly prayed for an outpouring of God's Spirit. As they got their church involved, they prayed the power of heaven down, and God sent Duncan Campbell to help birth a revival that shook the world. It's said that men aboard ships who passed the harbor fell under the conviction of the Holy Spirit and cried out to God for mercy. People in the streets fell to their knees in repentance before God receiving His salvation. Work stopped. Bars closed. Crime ceased.

Heaven's power knows no age limits, and Heaven's power is desperately needed today in the church and our nation. Prayer and fasting invite God's intervention in the affairs of mankind on earth.

You may feel like you're too old or unqualified or sense no special spiritual calling to do anything for God and His Kingdom. But you can serve God with fasting and prayer. You can pray for a Spirit of holiness to come upon the church once again and for lukewarm Christians to be set on fire by God's Holy Spirit. You can fast and pray for our nation to turn back to God. Your heart can be fully devoted to God as Simeon's was. As Anna's was.

I believe that someday, at the judgment seat of Christ where rewards are given out, the highest honors will not go to well-known evangelists, or prophets, or teachers, or pastors, but to those who, in obscurity, served God with fasting and prayer. Especially the "old" who got to be in on God's "new."

Scripture to meditate:

- Matthew 6:6: "But you, when you pray, go into your room, and when you have shut your door, pray to your Father who is in the secret place; and your Father who see in secret will reward you openly."

Perhaps you want to give up eating certain things or watching certain television programs as a fast unto God, and pray for God's Kingdom to come, for His will to be done in the church and our nation. Write your thoughts here.

_____

_____

38

Marriage Bedrock

I've been asked by several women how Dave's and my marriage has lasted fifty years. Seems it's a rarity these days. A woman I'll name Roxy told me she knows of a pastor's daughter who got married and divorced all in the space of one month and that she isn't the only one! What? Something is crazy, seriously wrong with that picture! God hates divorce, and it should not happen! Let me share some thoughts for a solid foundation for marriage.

1. Be selective in your dating.

The time to prepare for a solid marriage is when you're dating. Whom you choose to date is extremely important! God says in Amos 3:3, "Can two walk together, unless they are agreed?" Find out if they are a sincere follower of Jesus; don't date someone who will lead you away from your love and obedience to the Lord. If you want a marriage that lasts, both husband and wife must start with a solid foundation, and honor God's word as the plumb line for life. I have heard more than one story of trouble and heartbreak from women because they thought they could change their boyfriend after they got married. You'll save yourself and your family a lot of trouble. Remember: when you marry someone, you also, in a very real sense, marry their family.

Jesus says, "Anyone who listens to my teaching and follows it is wise, like a person who builds a house on solid rock. Though the rain comes in torrents and the floodwaters rise and the winds beat against that house, it won't collapse because it is built on bedrock. But anyone who hears my teaching and ignores it is foolish, like a person who builds a house on sand. When the rains and floods come, and the winds beat against that house, it will collapse with a mighty crash" (Matthew 7:24 – 27, NLT).

2. Commit to sexual purity when dating (and after you're married).

My mother instilled in me the virtues of sexual purity and proper behavior toward the opposite sex, and Dave and I obeyed our parents' dating guidelines. Even though we didn't like it, we respected our parents' wishes to not see one another but once a week, and that was on Sunday evenings when he brought me home after church. I was a senior in high school, and Dave had quit school because he hated it and wanted to help his dad work on the farm instead (he later got his GED certificate.) We wrote notes back and forth several times a week, with his twin brother Jonathan acting as mail carrier. So, we didn't even see one another in school. Dave did take me to our youth group activities (he went to a different Mennonite church than I) and sang in our youth choir; I saw him on those occasions.

We had no television, didn't go to the movies or go bowling, because as Mennonites, we didn't believe a Christian should do those things. On a typical Sunday night date, after we came to my home after church, we joined the family in the kitchen for snacks, and Mom always had good things set out to eat. Sometimes we worked on a puzzle at the dining room table with my parents and four brothers or played a board game. When the family went to bed, Dave and I usually had an hour or so alone together when we listened to LP records as we sat on the living room couch and sometimes held hands. As we listened, we talked about such things as our commitment to sexual purity (yes, we discussed it!) and love for the Lord, sermons and scriptures that were meaningful to us, school, and family happenings. (More than once my youngest brother, George, was caught peeking around the corner at us before Mom made him go back to bed.)

After six months of dating, I had my first kiss (on my forehead) as Dave was leaving for home at 10:30 one Sunday night. When I kissed him back on the cheek, he told me later he floated home.

In warmer weather, we took walks on the farm. Talking about our commitment to stay sexually pure guarded us against yielding to temptation and gave us deep respect for one another. Young people need to commit to proper behavior before temptation strikes, so they will be prepared to stay pure. And that only comes by placing a great value on the word of God. "How shall a young man cleanse his way? By taking heed and keeping watch [on himself] according to Your word [conforming his life to it]" (Psalm 119:9, Amplified Bible).

Promiscuity before or after marriage robs the marriage bed of sacred joy. But let me hasten to add that for those who have been promiscuous, there is forgiveness and healing through Jesus. If you're dating (or married) and have succumbed to sexual sin, acknowledge your sin, receive your forgiveness in Jesus, change your thinking, and stop the behavior. But it's so much better not to have to deal with memories of sin and wrong-doing in the first place.

I'm very concerned that too much of the church has succumbed to the culture of the world that treats sex as a recreational sport. That mindset needs to change. Your body is not your own; it belongs to God if you're a Christian. God created the sexual experience to be a spiritual and emotional bond between husband and wife; it's sacred and must be treated as such.

Over the years, Dave and I also attended marriage retreats where we learned life skills in communication and conflict resolution. Understanding your mate by being aware of the differences between male and female thinking are also vital necessities for building a lasting marriage. There are numerous Christian books and resources available on these subjects.

Scripture to meditate:

- Hebrews 13:4: "Marriage is honorable among all, and the bed undefiled; but fornicators and adulterers God will judge."
- Proverbs 5:15 – 21: "Drink water from your own cistern and running water from your own well. Should your fountains be dispersed abroad, streams of water in the streets? Let them be only your own, and not for strangers with you. Let your fountain be blessed and rejoice with the wife of your youth. As a loving deer and a graceful doe, let her breasts satisfy you at all times; and always be enraptured with her love. For why should you, my son, be enraptured by an immoral woman, and be embraced in the arms of a seductress? For the ways of man are before the eyes of the Lord, and He ponders all his paths."

How is God speaking to you today?

_____

_____

39

Marriage Building

Many couples make the mistake of viewing their wedding day as the most important part of their marriage, and have the attitude, "If it doesn't work out, we can always get divorced." If you want a blessed marriage, don't use Hollywood and prenuptial agreements for a template! How secure would you feel in a relationship if your fiancé insisted on a pre-nup? Think about that. It's the seedbed for divorce.

The couple needs to make sure they are on the same page spiritually and have the Lord at the center of their marriage. Couples should discuss their expectations and goals for marriage. As Dave and I recently read our love letters from fifty-two years ago, I was struck by how we began each letter with either a Scripture or a verse of good poetry, and how we continually talked about the Lord and His importance in our lives. Trust in, and commitment to, one another and to the Lord are absolutes in building a life-long, happy marriage.

You'll notice I said, "building." The survival of your building (as in *The Three Little Pigs*) depends on your building material: straw, sticks or bricks. Flimsy building materials include selfishness, blaming, unforgiveness, anger, attempts at controlling the other, jealousy, unresolved arguments, the silent treatment...you get the idea. Those materials are straw and sticks—fire starters—and that big, bad wolf will burn your house to the ground.

In an atmosphere thick and tight with frustration, resentment, and anger, as you wait for the other to apologize and break the standoff, you'll get on a destructive, never-ending crazy cycle that spins out of control. If you don't break that crazy cycle, you will likely end up in divorce court. Let me suggest that whoever fancies himself as the most spiritual makes the first move toward reconciliation. Only those who yield to the Spirit of God can break such a situation. It's a position of power! (The big, bad wolf doesn't want you to think so.)

Personal choices are the building materials of your marriage. Build your house with bricks forged in the furnace of God's love by choosing humility and understanding. Like the little pig that built his house with bricks, your home will then withstand the storms of life and the onslaughts of the Devil, the "big bad wolf" who comes only to steal, kill, and destroy. Don't collect fire starters!

Dr. Emerson Eggerichs, author of *Love and Respect* marriage materials, says counselors and the church have made the mistake of focusing only on love in a marriage. Let me explain. Have you ever seen a Hallmark card for a husband that says, "I respect you?" If you have, I'd like to see it. I submit to you that in our love-dominated culture, those cards most likely all say, "I love you with all my heart" or a similar variety of expression of love for the husband or boyfriend. But guys feel loved when they know they are respected.

- Be kind to one another.
- Make it a habit to say "Please," and "Thank-you."
- Link arms; be a team.
- Look for the good in each other and give personal compliments often (even if you don't feel like it).
- Speak well of one another in public, as well as at home.
- Always be respectful of your spouse's ideas, time, energy, opinions, and preferences.
- Refuse to harbor a critical spirit.

- Guard the tone of your voice and watch your body language. Hands on the hips, a pointing finger and a sharp tongue tear down the walls of home sweet home.
- Be quick to apologize for your part in a hurtful argument or wrong-doing.
- Smile often, choose a cheerful attitude, speak a kind word of encouragement.
- Try to please one another; learn what makes a person feel loved and respected and do them!
- Never say the "D" word: divorce! Don't even think it!

I want to add one important caveat: my comments are not intended for those who are in a physically or emotionally-abusive marriage! In such circumstances, separate yourself from that abuse and get help! My remarks are intended to help fine-tune marriages that have gotten into a rut of neglect and disorder. There is no earthly blessing so great as a God-centered, peaceful marriage filled with joy and security!

Scripture to meditate:

- "However, let each man of you [without exception] love his wife as [being in a sense] his very own self, and let the wife see that she **respects** and reverences her husband [that she notices him, regards him, honors him, prefers him, venerates, and esteems him, and that she defers to him, praises him, and loves and admires him exceedingly" (Ephesians 5:33, Amplified Bible).
- I Peter 3:1-12

What is God speaking to you?

_____

_____

40

Love and Respect

Carrie:

Carrie gritted her teeth and slammed the dishes into the dishwasher. She couldn't believe Trent would be so insensitive on her birthday! Not that he noticed—he never even mentioned her it. Why didn't he take her out to dinner to celebrate? Instead, he even turned on the television to watch an episode of M*A*S*H during dinner. She felt like she could m-a-s-h him.

She brushed away angry tears as she furiously wiped the table and countertops and glanced at Trent settled comfortably in his favorite chair watching television and reading the newspaper. How could he take her so for granted? Look at him: taking it easy while she was still slaving away, cleaning up after a dinner she shouldn't have had to make in the first place.

Carrie made up her mind not to say anything. She would be noble and suffer in silence. This wasn't the first time she felt disappointed with Trent. Why couldn't he treat her like he used to when they were dating? He was so attentive and thoughtful then.

Trent:

Trent peered at Carrie over the newspaper. Why did she act so strange? She hardly said a word during dinner, and the sound of dishes flung into the dishwasher alerted him that something was up. He noticed her deep sigh and flushed cheeks. Was she angry about something?

She seemed a lot different lately. His mind went back to last week when Justin and Marybeth came over to watch a movie, and he'd cringed with embarrassment as Carrie put him down in front of his friends. She criticized what he was wearing and talked about how he snored when he slept. She said he was too outspoken in their life group at church and that he walked through the house like a blundering moose.

Maybe her mood tonight had something to do with that diet book he gave her last month. . . He sighed and focused his attention back on the television. There'd be no romance in this house tonight.

What's going on here? According to Dr. Emerson Eggerichs' book, "Love and Respect," Carrie and Trent got themselves on the Crazy Cycle and can't seem to get off. It goes something like this: because she feels unloved, Carrie reacts to Trent without respect; without respect from Carrie, Trent reacts to her without love. Is there a way off this destructive merry-go-round? (Only it's not so "merry!)

Let's pretend Trent could see a picture of Carrie's emotional world. Love is the air she needs to breathe, and there's an imaginary hose connected to her love tank. When Trent steps on her air hose, Carrie feels unloved. If Carrie could see Trent's need to breathe the air of respect, she wouldn't be so quick to step on the air hose attached to his love tank and make him feel disrespected. When you see the spirit of the other deflate, and communication shuts down (or maybe a royal verbal battle ensues), you would know you are stepping on the other's air hose. Don't exercise squatter's rights: get off!

"Well," you may ask, "Who's to get off first?" Here's some good advice: the one who considers himself the most spiritual goes first. Humility and good communication skills are keys in "clearing the air." Blame-placing only makes the crazy cycle spin faster.

Maybe you don't know what to say. Here are some dialog openers you may find helpful:

- The husband could say to his wife, "I feel disrespected. Did I come across to you as unloving just now?"
- And the wife could say to her husband, "That felt unloving to me. Did I just come across as disrespectful toward you?"

Dr. Eggerichs describes the energizing cycle: his love motivates her respect, and her respect motivates his love. That wheel will take you in the direction you want to go!

Husband, speak kindly to your wife and encourage her. Speak well of her and keep her faults between the two of you. Shield and protect your wife from physical harm and verbal abuse of others. Thank her for the good things she does, build her up, and value her.

Learn what things make your spouse feel loved or respected, whether it's receiving gifts, words of affirmation, touch, acts of service, or quality time. If you don't know your love language, I recommend both husband and wife take this quiz on Gary Chapman's website at http://www.5lovelanguages.com/, and let each other know what yours is.

Both husband and wife should practice being cheerful and friendly. I wonder how much marital trouble could be avoided if they each would just smile at the other! Guard your marriage by refusing to take offense and allowing it to fester.

Wife, brag about your husband's good points to others and speak well of him. Tell him his faults in private if you must, but don't ever despise him in your heart. Thank him for doing things for you and don't take him for granted. Comment on things well done. Do things that you know make him feel respected.

Scripture to mediate:

- "The heart of her husband safely trusts her, so he will have no lack of gain. She does him good and not evil all the days of his life" (Proverbs 31:11 – 12).

- Ephesians 5:33: "However, let each man of you [without exception] love his wife as [being in a sense] his very own self; and let the wife see that she respects and reverences her husband [that she notices him, regards him, honors him, prefers him, venerates him, and esteems him; and that she defers to him, praises him, and loves and admires him exceedingly] (Ephesians 5:33, Amplified Bible).

- "Has not the Lord made them one? In flesh and spirit they are his. And why one? Because he was seeking godly offspring. So guard yourself in your spirit, and do not break faith with the wife of your youth. 'I hate divorce', says the Lord God of Israel, 'and I hate a man's covering himself with violence as well as with his garment', says the Lord Almighty. So guard yourself in your spirit and do not break faith" (Malachi 2:15 – 16, NIV).

What is God speaking to you today?

_____

_____

41

A Softened Heart

"I'm not going to your parents' house for Thanksgiving, and that's that!" Nancy's eyes threw daggers at her husband as she sat down to watch television.

Frank sighed and threw up his hands. They'd had this argument the past two years ever since Nancy had a falling-out with his mother. Frank knew his mom spoke her mind, and he'd talked to her about the way she'd hurt Nancy's feelings. His mother tried to apologize to Nancy, but his wife closed her heart.

"Nancy, I miss not spending Thanksgiving with my parents; why can't you understand that? How would you feel if I refused to go to your parents' home for Christmas?" Frank appealed. Lord knows he'd prayed a lot about Nancy's attitude toward his mom.

Nancy didn't answer but clicked on the television. The first words she heard startled her: "Wives, submit to your husbands as to the Lord. For the husband is the head of the wife as Christ is the head of the church, his body, of which he is the Savior. Now as the church submits to Christ, so also wives should submit to their husbands in everything. Husbands, love your wives, just as Christ loved the church and gave himself up for her…"

The minister went on to say, "This scripture from Ephesians 5: 21 to 33 talks about how husbands and wives need to submit to one another. The husband must love his wife as he loves himself and the wife must respect her husband. We read the same instruction in Titus 2 verse 5 that wives are to be subject to their own husbands, so the word of God will not be ill-spoken of."

Frank saw Nancy's finger hover over the remote to change channels, but for some reason she kept listening.

"Let's not forget Ephesians 5:21 that says we are to submit to one another out of reverence for Christ. The teaching that wives must submit to their husbands has been very misunderstood and abused in some Christian circles. Sometimes people get the idea that women are basically to be a doormat or a robot for their husbands, while the husband is given unlimited authority over his wife. Despite this distorted teaching, we cannot get around the fact that the Lord did say through Paul that wives are to submit to their own husbands. Just because a teaching isn't popular is no reason to discard it. Indeed, we dare not."

The speaker continued, "Second Timothy 3:16 tells us that all Scripture is God-breathed and is useful for teaching, rebuking, correcting and training in righteousness. We need to humble our hearts to the Lord to be taught by Him. The word of God teaches that the husband is the head of the home, and the wife should respect his role. The husband should understand that such leadership requires service—he is to be a 'servant-leader!' The wife should willingly submit to her husband's God-given role and not try to upstage him. The truth is, they are to submit to one another as they submit to Christ in their lives. The husband is to love his wife, and the wife is to respect her husband. This is pleasing to the Lord."

Nancy turned the television off and looked over at Frank. He saw her face soften. "I'm sorry, Frank; I've not been respectful of your leadership. Please forgive me."

Frank never felt more loved by his wife than at the moment they embraced.

Nancy reached for the phone. "Call your mother and tell her we accept her invitation to spend Thanksgiving with them."

Scripture to Meditate:

- "Therefore, just as the church is subject to Christ, so let the wives be to their own husbands in everything. Husbands, love your wives, just as Christ loved the church, and gave Himself for her" (Ephesians 5:24 – 25).

What is God saying to you?

_____

_____

42

Submission: A
Dirty Word?

A scripture that has helped my husband and me relate properly to one another is Ephesians 5:33, and I'll quote it from the Amplified Bible. The Apostle Paul was talking about how marriage between a man and a woman typifies Christ and the Church, for he says in verses 25 and 26 of the same chapter, "Husbands, love your wives, as Christ loved the church and gave Himself up for her, so that He might sanctify her, having cleansed her by the washing of water with the Word."

Verse 33 says, "However, let each man of you [without exception] love his wife as [being in a sense] his very own self; and let the wife see that she respects and reverences her husband [that she notices him, regards him, honors him, prefers him, venerates, and esteems him; and that she defers to him, praises him, and loves and admires him exceedingly.]"

First Peter 3: 1 – 2 (Amplified Bible) agrees: "In like manner, you married women, be submissive to your own husbands [subordinate yourselves as being secondary to and dependent on them, and adapt yourselves to them], so that even if any do not obey the Word [of God], they may be won over not by discussion but by the [godly] lives of their wives, when they observe the pure and modest way in which you conduct yourselves, together with your reverence [for your husband; you are to feel for him all that reverence includes: to respect, defer to, revere him—to honor, esteem, appreciate, prize, and, in the human sense, to adore him, that is, to admire, praise, be devoted to, deeply love, and enjoy your husband]."

Submission is a dirty word to many, but we need a proper Christian understanding of it. Notice the command is to be submissive to your own husband—not someone else's. Don't value another man's words above your husband's. And submission does not mean that you let your husband walk all over you or mistreat you. I found it very helpful to understand what the Holy Spirit means by "reverence" for my husband. It simply means to:

- Notice him: look at him when he speaks or enters a room; learn to read his signals.
- Prefer him: give him the best slice of meat, the biggest piece of dessert, the un-chipped glass.
- Venerate him: regard him with respect.
- Esteem him: set a high value on him.
- Defer to him: let him make the final decision on a matter after you've given your input.
- Praise him: compliment him privately and in public; brag on him.
- Adore him: be extremely fond of him and honor him.
- Love him: have a warm attachment and devotion to him.
- Admire him: marvel at his accomplishments, regard him with admiration.
- Be devoted to him: be loyal to him; set your heart apart from all others for him.
- Enjoy him: have a good time with him; play together.
- Prize him: consider him as one who is exceptionally desirable.

One might think, "But wouldn't I be lying if I do these things when I don't see my husband as worthy of my honor?" However, consider that God's word says if your husband is acting like a "bone-head," he will be won over by the way you treat him, not by nagging. The movie *Fireproof* demonstrates this.

God's says that by choosing to act a certain way, it's possible to change both your feelings and your husband's behavior. It's called "giving grace" where it's not deserved. That's how God treats us. A lot of food for thought here.

Anti-cultural, I know; but I'm sticking with the word of God.

How can you give grace to that special someone in your life?

_____

_____

43

Mirror, Mirror, on the Wall

That pesky, negative self-image! Why does it seem to follow us around? Can you relate? We know we do most things well, but when we make a mistake, or someone makes one negative comment about us, our spirits sink. We can succumb to guilt, heap blame on ourselves, and wallow in misery for hours, or even days. We can feel unworthy of being loved (or even given grace by God) and makes it hard to believe we are worthy of a compliment.

It's true we are not to brag on ourselves, for Scripture says, "Let another praise you, and not your own mouth; someone else, and not your own lips" (Proverbs 27:2). But as Christians, we should have a sanctified self-image, and learn to receive compliments with humility.

I've heard that in Japanese culture, if someone is given a compliment they quickly say, "It's nothing—It's nothing!" And if you leave a tip in a restaurant in Japan, they are highly insulted because they interpret that to mean they haven't done a good job in serving you. Interesting.

Recently a friend on Facebook addressed a comment to me: "Mom can never seem to be able to enjoy her own food. She always frets about it and is convinced it didn't turn out good (though it's always delicious).

This mother would graciously give kindness to other cooks who thought their food was not good and find something encouraging to say. Why not treat herself as she would the other person? Something to think about.

Perfectionist tendencies make us so self-critical. It's okay to not be perfect! The Lord knows I'm not, but I decided several years ago to like "me" anyway! Sometimes cooking for others is a way we show love, and when the product doesn't meet our own high standards and expectations, we subconsciously feel a loss of self-worth. We put a lot of pressure on ourselves.

Sometimes a mom or dad thinks they are showing love to a son our daughter by continually pointing out their faults. One such young man, when asked to describe his mother, said she was disapproving, demanding, impatient and unreasonable—hard to please. He had become a driven perfectionist who felt he could never please God or be close to him. Parents can criticize their children to the point of exasperating them, making them feel like a hopeless failure. Ephesians 6:4 reads, "Father's, do not exasperate your children; instead, bring them up in the training and instruction of the Lord."

As you can see, what we experience as children affects our view of ourselves and, worst of all, our image of God—the only One who can change our self-image. We need to know how much He loves and accepts us, so we can accept ourselves. When someone gives us a compliment, we should humbly say, "Thank-you," instead of feeling embarrassed or confused about whether to accept or down-play the compliment lest we be perceived as prideful. When someone gives me a compliment, and I negate it, am I not telling the other person her opinion is worthless? How might that make her feel?

Also, if you repeat negative things about yourself, you reinforce those recorded thoughts and beliefs, kind of like worn grooves in an old LP album. If you're old enough to remember the phonograph, you'll remember how it sounded when the needle got stuck.

It seems we have somehow been subconsciously conditioned to be negative. We don't give ourselves permission to think of ourselves in a positive light. Romans 12:3 says to "not think of yourself more highly than you ought, but rather think of yourself with sober judgment." That is not saying you shouldn't think well of yourself. If you don't love yourself, how can you love your neighbor? You don't love yourself by focusing on your faults. And you don't love your neighbor by focusing on his, either. If you've been driven to perfectionism because of circumstances in your life, please know it's okay to give yourself a break for not doing things right all the time.

I once read the comment, "I can't afford to have any thoughts about me that God doesn't have," and I totally agree. God loves us unconditionally because He has chosen to give us grace. Freely you have received—freely give. Ask the Holy Spirit to help you give grace to yourself and enjoy your life as you rest in Him. Be of good cheer and meditate on how much God loves you.

Scripture to Meditate:

- "Grace to you and peace from God our Father, and the Lord Jesus Christ" (Ephesians 1:2).
- "But God, who is rich in mercy, because of His great love with which He loved us, even when we were dead in trespasses, made us alive together with Christ (by grace you have been saved), and raised us up together and made us sit together in the heavenly places in Christ Jesus, that in the ages to come He might show the exceeding riches of His grace in His kindness toward us in Christ Jesus (Ephesians 2:4 – 7).

What do you believe God thinks about you?

_____

_____

Sound Bites

It filled the news with sound bites. (And yes, sometimes I felt like biting back!) The childish bickering, finger-pointing and fault-finding by some of the political candidates who ran for the nomination for president of the United States was downright embarrassing and wearisome. Networks thrived on the debacle because it drew viewers. And because of high viewer exposure, those networks could charge higher prices for companies who wanted to advertise. In all my years, I had not heard such demeaning political rhetoric.

I understand the anger of we, the American people, who feel ripped off by our government, by insider politicians who talk a pretty talk, but don't walk the walk. A sea of broken promises, spineless compromise, and back-room deal-making contrary to the will of the electorate litter the political shore leaving in its dirty wake people whose religious freedoms are challenged, are forced out of business, have lost their jobs, and who are threatened by the very government that was supposed to provide freedom, protection, and justice for its citizenry.

I get it. I feel the same way. I agree we as Christian people need to be bolder to speak out for what is right and quit cowering to political correctness. But there's a right and a wrong way to do that. We can do it without speaking evil of those in office, or those running for office; we have an absolute right and responsibility to discuss issues, but we don't have a right to assassinate someone's character or judge their motives. We can have civil discourse on issues and try to find solutions rather than attack people. And most of all, we are commanded to pray.

I remember both times when President Obama was elected, I found it very hard to pray for him. I was angry and disappointed, and my heart felt a deep grief for our country and feared the destruction of the America I loved. Yet, I knew I was commanded to pray for him. I didn't want to do it, but because I loved Jesus, I did it. (Didn't Jesus say, "If you love me, keep My commandments?")

And when I heard there were threats against his life, I prayed for his safety and that of his family. I asked God to help me pray for him— from my heart. I had to come to the place where I saw President Obama as a man God loves as much as He loves me, who wanted him "to be saved and to come to the knowledge of the truth." When I thought of his eternal destiny, it was much easier to pray for him. It kept my mouth from uttering angry, destructive words against him.

When I pray, it also changes my heart, so I will have spiritual quiet, reverence, and godliness, regardless of what is going on in my natural world. On social media, I refused to "like" derogatory things said about President Obama. Discussing an issue and contending for the truth is always okay; personal attacks are not.

The Holy Spirit often talks to me when I do my hair and makeup in the morning. Recently He showed me how what we're seeing in this volatile political season reflects the condition of too much of the body of Christ. One denomination points the finger at another denomination; there's ridicule and demeaning talk against brothers and sisters in the Lord who worship and believe differently. My friends, these things should not be. How can we ever be salt and light to a needy, watching world, and do kingdom business in the name of the Lord, when we are dominated with an "us vs. them" attitude and speak evil of fellow brothers and sisters in the Lord? The Devil loves mayhem and laughs with glee at how people are clueless that they're pawns in his malicious hands to do his dirty work! When the body of Christ is busy finding fault, it is no threat to our enemy's kingdom.

James, the half- brother of Jesus, wrote in his letter to the church, ". . . Look also at ships: although they are so large and are driven by fierce winds, they are turned by a very small rudder wherever the pilot desires. Even so the tongue is a fire, a world of iniquity. The tongue is so set among our members that it defiles the whole body, and sets on fire the course of nature; and it is set on fire by hell. . . With it we bless our God and Father and with it we curse men, who have been made in the similitude of God. Out of the same mouth proceed blessing and cursing. My brethren, these things ought not to be so. Does a spring send forth fresh water and bitter from the same opening? Can a fig tree, my brethren, bear olives, or a grapevine bear figs? Thus, no spring yields both salt water and fresh" (James 3:4-12).

Scripture to Meditate:

- "Therefore, I exhort first of all that supplications, prayers, intercessions, and giving of thanks be made for all men, for kings and all who are in authority, that we may lead a quiet and peaceable life in all godliness and reverence. For this is good and acceptable in the sight of God our Savior, who desires all men to be saved and to come to the knowledge of the truth" (I Timothy 2:2 – 4).

Write a prayer for those in authority over us.

_____

_____

45

Sex Matters

I heard evangelist Perry Stone relay a young minister's account of how, after preaching in a church (that shall remain nameless) on a Sunday evening, the pastor of the church said, "You may not want to participate in the after-hour activities this evening." The young minister noticed that several couples were headed downstairs and asked the pastor what he meant by that comment. The pastor continued, "We have such liberty in Christ, that after service Sunday evenings, we go downstairs to watch X-rated movies and wife-swap." Gasp!

The young minister also told Perry another incident: "The next Sunday, I preached in another church, and while we were sitting on the platform, the pastor said to me, 'See that woman in the second row? I'm going to divorce my wife and marry her, because she's more profitable to the ministry.'" Double gasp!

Still not finished, the young minister told Perry yet another story: "The following Sunday evening, I spoke in a church and while on the platform, the pastor nudged me and said, 'See all those girls on the front row? I can arrange to have any one of them sent to your hotel room later.'" Triple gasp!

I was horrified as I heard these accounts. How can we expect our culture to change from darkness to light when we in the church engage in the world's practices? I have asked myself why it seems sexual sins are the only ones society targets for acceptance. There is such an agenda by the LBGT community (and now even pedophilia groups) to have the church approve of their lifestyles, and sexual confusion engulfs our young people as never before. Schools now teach children to choose their sexual identity. The results are tragic.

When Christians refuse to accept the sin as okay, we are called homophobic and other names. While I decry those Christians, who are unloving and obnoxious in speaking out against sexual sin, I will not ever agree that sex outside the design and plan of God is okay. It destroys individuals and the family unit, bringing much sorrow and heartache. God's word is the truth, and we believers are the salt of the earth—preservers of righteousness. We must learn how to hate the sin and still love those caught in sin. Jesus did, and we can too. He told the woman caught in adultery, "Neither do I condemn you; go and sin no more" (John 8:11). He didn't tell her she wasn't sinning.

I believe with all my heart that at some point in their lives, the precious people caught in the web of deviant sexual sin were infected by an unclean spirit. Because of misguided thinking, and the belief that "God controls everything," some Christians even say people are born homosexual and therefore it's "God's gift to them." Nothing could be further from the truth! A deviant spirit or other factors may have infected an infant or young child, but God did not make them that way. Let me be clear: deviant sexual desires are not a gift from God, and people can be set free of sexual confusion through deliverance in the name of Jesus. Satan is the author of confusion and every evil work.

My heart goes out to those caught in sexual confusion and a deviant lifestyle; I want so much for them to be set free by the power of Jesus. There is forgiveness and freedom available! I recommend the book, *Called Out* by a former lesbian, Janet Boynes. With helpful compassion, she tells her own story how, as a young Christian, she got on the wrong track. She describes her dysfunctional home life and her eventual journey to freedom from a lesbian lifestyle. It's an excellent book for anyone wanting to help others caught in sexual confusion.

We must never conclude it's okay for anyone to live a sexually-deviant lifestyle. Sin is sin, no matter if it's lying, stealing, abuse, adultery, fornication, you name it. Jesus died and rose again to give us freedom from sin, and He loves everyone. Let's hold out the beacon of love, light and truth to a society steeped in deception. Amen.

Scripture to Meditate:

- "Flee sexual immorality. Every sin a man does is outside the body, but he who commits sexual immorality sins against his own body. Or do you not know that your body is the temple of the Holy Spirit who is in you, whom you have from God, and you are not your own? For you were bought with a price; therefore, glorify God in your body and in your spirit, which are God's" (I Corinthians 6:18 – 20).
- "Each of you should know how to possess his own vessel in sanctification and honor, not in passion or lust, like the Gentiles who do not know God. . . For God did not call us to uncleanness, but in holiness. Therefore, he who rejects this does not reject man, but God, who has also given us His Holy Spirit" (I Thessalonians 4:4, 7 – 8).
- "Therefore, God also gave them up to uncleanness, in the lusts of their hearts, to dishonor their bodies among themselves, who exchanged the truth of God for the lie, and worshiped and served the creature rather than the Creator, who is blessed forever, Amen. For this reason, God gave them up to vile passions. For even their women exchanged the natural use for what is against nature. Likewise, also the men, leaving the natural use of the woman, burned in their lust for one another, men with men committing what is shameful, and receiving in themselves the penalty of their error which was due" (Romans 1:24 – 27).

Declare: I will honor God with my body.

Write a prayer of hope and deliverance for someone you know who is caught in sexual sin, or for someone who is deceived into believing sexual sin is okay.

46

Giants and Grasshoppers

The Bible tells how Moses sent spies into the Israelite's promised land, Canaan; but fearful men spread a bad report about the land and said, "We even saw giants there, the descendants of Anak. Next to them we felt like grasshoppers, and that's what they thought, too! (Numbers 13: 33, NLT). God was quite angry with them for being fearful, and those who were afraid died off in the desert and never did get to enjoy the land the Lord intended to give them. Of all the original group of Israelites, only Joshua and Caleb got to see the fulfillment of God's promise.

We have our personal giants in our lives to conquer, and no matter the issue, God says He always causes us to triumph in Christ Jesus (2 Corinthians 2:14). God has sent the Church on a mission as well, to be wise as serpents and harmless as doves (Matthew 10:16), to impact our culture with the Kingdom of Heaven (Matthew 6:10), to teach and make disciples of all nations (Matthew 28:19 – 20).

Our culture can look big, bad, and scary as foundations of society crumble around us. Truthfully, the Church too often has been self-absorbed, passive, and easily intimidated by loud voices that try to discourage and silence us from speaking out on moral issues. The Church has let too much of the world creep in and take over its thinking. Little by little, we have retreated with the hope that the world will finally like us if we keep quiet. To me, the expression, "Can't we just all get along?" too often means, "Just agree; there's no absolute truth. And for Pete's sake, don't cause dissent." My friend, the truth is, someone's values and decisions will always prevail. No, phrases like the preceding one are calculated to shut up the righteous, cut off their influence from society, and promote an agenda contrary to the word of God. Jesus said, "In this world you will have tribulation, but be of good cheer: I have overcome the world" (John 16:33).

It may seem like the devil's side is winning the day but make no mistake: God has already won. I love Revelation 11:15: "Then the seventh angel sounded: and there were loud voices in heaven saying, 'The kingdoms of this world have become the kingdoms of our Lord and of His Christ, and He shall reign forever and ever!'"

My friend, let's not be passive or retreat from the truth. In our spiritual warfare, we fight from a place of rest in the finished work of Jesus and the authority He has given us. Let's run toward the battle; let's invade the darkness!

When we know who we are in Jesus, we won't feel helpless in conquering our own giants, nor feel like grasshoppers next to a big, bad, scary, giant of a decaying culture. Let's search for the souls of men and women, boys and girls, and rescue those who are perishing. Let's bring life and freshness, hope and healing! My heart's desire is to learn to love more perfectly and do the works of Jesus by putting action to my faith in His gospel: "As you go, preach, saying, 'The kingdom of heaven is at hand.' Heal the sick, raise the dead, cast off demons. Freely you have received, freely give" (Matthew 10:8). Let us give Jesus the reward for His suffering! As the simple scripture song says so well, "Be bold; be strong, for the Lord our God is with you!"

Read Ephesians 6:10 – 18) that lists our armor for standing firm in the day of battle.

Scripture to Meditate:

- John 15:18-19: "If the world hates you, you know that it hated Me before it hated you. If you were of the world, the world would love its own. Yet because you are not of this world, but I chose you out of the world, therefore the world hates you" (John 15:18 – 19).

Declare: "I can do all things through Christ Who strengthens me" (Philippians 4:13).

Where do you need God's strength today?

_____

_____

47

The Little White Church on Beachley Street

Feelings of wistful sadness washed over me as I lay sleepless. I thought of the small white church I attended as a pre-teen and teen: First Mennonite Church on Beachley Street in Meyersdale, Pennsylvania. My throat tightened as memories crowded my mind.

I visualized the center row of long dark benches and two rows of shorter dark benches on either side, creating two aisles. At the age of eleven, I had stood at the end of one of those center benches to publicly declare my faith in Jesus Christ as tears rolled down my face. And after several weeks of instruction, I knelt in front of that church to be baptized by the Mennonite method of pouring.

I remembered a row of benches against the back wall of the church, too. I saw the pulpit and the two alcove windows behind the pulpit in front, with a picture of Jesus praying in the Garden of Gethsemane hanging on a narrow wall between the windows. I remember a door to the outside on the left. A steeple with a church bell that rang on Sundays graced the church over the entryway. Tall, narrow, frosted-glass windows looked like those of churches one sees on Christmas cards.

I thought about how that little church gave me the opportunity to develop in my Christian walk. Here in this place, I was asked to teach summer Bible School, Sunday school, and sometimes, along with others, give talks on certain topics Sunday nights.

We had a great youth chorus under the direction of Ray Hershberger, the father of my best friend Maretta. I remember the weekly practices and chorus programs we gave in churches and at Oakland Nursing Home in Maryland. I think we sounded quite good!

I recalled the wonderful youth group we had under the direction of Sam and Elizabeth Yoder. We held elections for a president, secretary and treasurer and followed Robert's Rules of Order in conducting our youth meetings. I remembered the mystery suppers, talent nights, hayrides and hot dog roasts, making food baskets at Thanksgiving for needy families, making candy in Elizabeth's (and my mom's) kitchens for Christmas packages, and more.

I'll never forget my impression of a preacher from the Church of the Nazarene who came to First Mennonite to preach for us. I can still see him walk to the platform, get down on his knees, and pray for a little while before preaching.

I remembered Ressley Tressler, Norman Teague and Ross Metzler who pastored our little church over the years. I gave thanks to God for their faithful oversight of our little flock.

When the church disbanded, a group of Spirit-filled "Amish Mennonites" started a Charismatic church there called Rock Church, and my husband and I were so blessed to be part of that. During that time, our first son was born, and we dedicated him to the Lord in the little white church. My parents and Dave's parents also attended there, and I thank God for their godly influence in our lives.

We drove past the little white church several years ago. That once-special place is now used for some sort of garage or tire storage facility and the windows are boarded shut. Overgrown with vines, trees, and shrubs that threaten the thirsty, once-white clapboard siding, my dear little church looked forlorn and badly neglected. I wiped my tears with the bed sheet. Even though the church is no more, it was once used by God to nurture me. I felt deeply grateful to God for all the people who entered and exited the doors of that little white church on Beachley Street.

Being part of a church fellowship is vital for Christian growth and safeguards our walk with the Lord. It's good for us to think back to where we first accepted Jesus' salvation, and gave our lives to Him. May our hearts always be tender toward Him. "The lines have fallen to me in pleasant places; yes, I have a good inheritance" (Psalm 16:6).

Scripture to Meditate:

- "I was glad when they said to me, 'Let us go into the house of the Lord'" (Psalm 122:1).
- "And let us consider one another in order to stir up love and good works, not forsaking the assembling of ourselves together, as is the manner of some, but exhorting one another, and so much more as you see the Day approaching" (Hebrews 10:24 – 24).

Write a prayer of thanksgiving to God for those who helped you on your spiritual journey.

_____

_____

48 ♡

Loneliness

Several years ago, my mom and I visited a facility that housed elderly residents here in Virginia. I remember the smells, the lonely looks in the eyes of those with nothing to do, sitting in wheel chairs parked alongside hallways. A few reached out a feeble hand as if to ask for help or to feel someone's touch. Most of them looked up at us with dull eyes that spoke of resignation and hopelessness—and utter loneliness.

There are many people at work, walk the streets, sit in our churches, shop in grocery stores, or sit around a family table who feel the pain of loneliness. Sometimes those who seem to be the "life of the party" in a crowd or who are the "social butterfly," are the loneliest of all when they slip between the bedsheets at night. Alone, and forgotten.

Lucy feels alone in her marriage. She and her husband, Brandon, live in a gorgeous home, and as the CEO of his own company he makes a great income. Work keeps him occupied seven days a week while Lucy tries to fill her lonely days with shopping, watching television, going out with friends or attending a Bible study. When she comes home from church, she either eats alone at home or in a restaurant, because Brandon is engrossed in his work or busy watching television.

Paula's husband comes home from work, eats dinner, then flops in his easy chair where he falls asleep watching television. She and Rob don't really have any friends, and they never go out. So, she tries to find solace in reading myriads of books and taking online courses to pass the lonely evening hours. She feels isolated.

Gary feels lonely when his wife, Susan, expects him to get his own dinner, then chooses to spend evenings at the computer or go out bowling with her friends instead of taking some time to sit with him while he watches a football game. He feels lonely when she criticizes and disrespects him, especially in front of others.

Dan says ever since the baby came, Nancy has no time for him. She gives much attention to the baby, and expects him to do his share of feeding, diapering and laundry, which he is glad to do. But Nancy seems to only be tuned to the baby's needs, and she forgets about his need for companionship and romance.

Sometimes even our children go through periods of loneliness when they feel they have no one to play with; they can feel excluded from others, especially if the family moves to a new area and school district. Or they may feel lonely when they lose a pet or special possession, and most definitely when they lose a friend, parent or grandparent. It's sad when children feel lonely because they feel rejected of unloved by their parents. Could it be that the bullies in our schools are products of such homes? Could it be that these kids become high school drop-outs, begin a life of delinquency, and grow up to be a liability to society and our already burgeoning prisons?

It's imperative that we parents keep open hearts, eyes, and ears to the facial expressions, words and behavior of our children. Don't let the pressures of life make you see your children as a bother rather than a blessing. Your child will surely pick up on your attitude and feel distanced from you. How can he feel free to talk to you if he feels he's just in your way and you have no time for him? You may provide the best clothes, food, and house money can buy, but if your child doesn't feel valued or cherished, it means little to him. What he wants and needs is understanding and acceptance, a loving touch and words spoken with kindness and reassurance.

We all have a fundamental need for friends, close relationships and inclusion in a group. Without that, people can fall apart mentally and physically. I love the Father's heart shown toward us in this Scripture: "A father to the fatherless, defender of widows is God in His holy dwelling. God sets the lonely in families; He leads forth the prisoners with singing" (Psalm 68:5 – 6).

People are the most valuable and important treasure on this earth. If you sense someone is withdrawn or lonely, have the love and courage to ask them if they're okay. Look to the interests of others and bear their burdens. Someone needs to care! You never know what a phone call, a kind smile, a cheerful conversation, or a light touch on an arm or shoulder can do for someone.

Proverbs 18:24 says, "A man who has friends must himself be friendly, but there is a friend who sticks closer than a brother." Jesus is that friend! And we need to be "Jesus with skin on" to others, too.

Scripture to Meditate:

- Galatians 6:2: "Carry each other's burdens, and in this way, you will fulfill the law of Christ."
- Philippians 2:4: "Each of you should look not only to your own interests but also to the interests of others."

Can you think of someone who seems lonely? How can you make a difference?

_____

_____

49

Why Work?

If one takes the book of Ecclesiastes in the Bible at face value, we would think work is meaningless—a miserable business at best. Poor King Solomon (though he was the wealthiest and wisest man who ever lived) spoke these words when he was depressed as he considered the whole of his life's achievements. He even said work was meaningless (Ecclesiastes 2: 17 – 26).

But work that benefits others is an honorable thing in God's sight. Colossians 3:23 (NIV) says, "Whatever you do, work at it with all your heart, as working for the Lord, not for men, since you know that you will receive an inheritance from the Lord as a reward." When one is focused on self, as King Solomon was in his writing of Ecclesiastes, work is meaningless and unfulfilling.

Moms, when you drive to your job to endure office politics one more day, remember why you do what you do. When you put one more load of laundry into the washer, dust that furniture one more time, sweep and mop the floors, remember why you do what you do. When you prepare your thousandth meal, wash the dishes one more time, run those household errands, kneel beside a sick child's bed (again), when weariness and sleeplessness stalks you like an enemy, remember why you do what you do.

Dads, when you brave the ice and snow, fix that broken washer or dryer, take risks in starting a new business, mow the grass or take the car to the garage rather than sit down to watch television, remember why you do what you do. When you take your family to church rather than sleep in or help your child with homework instead of reading the newspaper, remember why you do what you do. When you help your neighbor start his car or shovel a sidewalk packed with snow, even though you're tired, remember why you do what you do.

What's the point of work anyway? What's the big deal? It's a very big deal. Look at it this way: imagine if nobody in society did anything but sit around and waited for someone else to do something useful. What kind of world would we have? When we do honorable work, we gain self- esteem, not by being given handouts, but by providing goods and services for others. As we bless others, we in turn bless our Creator God—our God of beauty and order. Our homes, communities, and our country should reflect that as well.

Too often, our welfare system promotes laziness and an ongoing generational dependence on a lifestyle of handouts from the government. If a person is able, he/she needs to seek gainful employment. Work is a godly thing!

Scripture to Meditate:

- "Make it your ambition to lead a quiet life, to mind your own business and to work with your own hands, just as we told you, so that your daily life may win the respect of outsiders and so that you will not be dependent on anybody" (I Thessalonians 4:11 – 12).
- "Now we ask you, brothers, to respect those who work hard among you, who are over you in the Lord and who admonish you. Hold them in the highest regard in love because of their work. Live in peace with each other. And we urge you, brothers,

warn those who are idle, encourage the timid, help the weak, be patient with everyone" (I Thessalonians 5:12 – 14, NIV).

- "In the name of the Lord Jesus Christ, we command you, brothers, to keep away from every brother who is idle and does not live according to the teaching you received from us. For you yourselves know how you ought to follow our example. We were not idle when we were with you, nor did we eat anyone's food without paying for it. On the contrary, we worked night and day, laboring and toiling so that we would not be a burden to any of you. We did this, not because we do not have the right to such help, but in order to make ourselves a model for you to follow. For even when we were with you, we gave you this rule: 'If a man will not work, he shall not eat'" (2 Thessalonians 3:6 – 12, NIV).

What work do you enjoy? How can you improve your work attitude?

_____

_____

$\heartsuit{50}\heartsuit$

Celebrate Life

When I celebrated my 66th birthday, I got my ears pierced for the first time, was treated to lunch and dinner, given a big beautiful bouquet of flowers, a lovely "Grandma" plaque, and a $50 Amazon gift card besides lots of love, hugs and well-wishes from family and friends.

Several years ago, a lady told me in no uncertain tones that she refuses to celebrate her birthday because she had nothing to do with it. She pontificated, "Why celebrate my birthday as though I had something to do with it? I didn't plan it, had no part in it, so why should I act like it's a big deal?" Is she right? Are birthday celebrations a waste of time, money and energy?

The way I see it, remembering someone's beginning is what birthdays are all about. The day you were conceived in your mother's womb was a time of celebration for your parents, grandparents, aunts and uncles; then they rejoiced at the tiny new life that made its appearance on earth. Baby cards called you a bundle of joy, a precious life, a reason to celebrate, and your parents were congratulated.

Birthdays are a validation of one's identity and existence. It would be sad indeed to see someone for whom there is no birthday celebration. A celebration says, "I value you, God values you, and I'm glad you're on the planet!" Birthdays also make us think, "Who am I? Where am I in life?"

But having a birthday isn't all about oneself. Celebrating a birthday bonds family and friends; our life story is part of another's. We remember our families are worth loving and want to do something nice for them on their birthday.

Life is precious, created by God. That's why abortion is so wrong; it's murder of an innocent life, which begins exactly at conception. The teeny person only needs nutrition and time to fully develop to the point of being able to survive outside the womb. God has a purpose and plan for everyone, even for those whose birth circumstances may have been far less than idyllic. No matter your circumstance at birth, God gave you special gifts and abilities that are unique to you. You fill a place on earth that nobody else can fill. You are a *somebody!* God didn't make a "nobody!"

Children especially look forward to celebrating their birthdays each year; they are eager for that birthday party and gifts. It's refreshing to see the exuberance of a child. Celebrations are like the exclamation points of life. Do you find it difficult to celebrate? Sometimes I think we adults let the devil suck the joy out of life. We have a hard time celebrating anything because we focus our attention on worries, guilt, lack of finances, mistakes, and "keeping our nose to the grindstone." There's an old saying, "All work and no play makes Jack a dull boy."

God wants us to enjoy life, to enjoy Him—to celebrate! The Old Testament has many commands for God's people to feast and celebrate His goodness. God delights in His creation; He needs you here on earth to be His hands and feet, His mouth, to bless others.

Scripture to Meditate:

- John 10:10: "The thief does not come except to steal, and to kill, and to destroy. I have come that they may have life, and that they may have it more abundantly."

- I Timothy 6:17: "God gives us richly all things to enjoy."
- "For you created my inmost being; you knit me together in my mother's womb. I praise you because I am fearfully and wonderfully made; your works are wonderful, I know that full well. My frame was not hidden from you when I was made in the secret place. When I was woven together in the depths of the earth, your eyes saw my unformed body. All the days ordained for me were written in your book before one of them came to be" (Psalm 139:13 – 16).

Where can you celebrate others as well as yourself?

_____

_____

51

Haste Makes Waste

Who hasn't experienced the consequences of impulsive, hasty actions? Sometimes I tend to be too hasty in acting on some things and don't deliberate or get advice before I act. I thank the Lord that He brought this to my attention, so I can make corrections.

There were a few times in the process of writing my first children's book where I was hasty. One such time was when I didn't take time to read the manuscript (for the tenth time, it seemed) slowly and deliberately, and it cost me lots of money with the publisher to go back and fix it later. A second pair of eyes would likely have caught errors I missed.

Have you made a hasty promise to somebody, including God, and then didn't keep your word? Maybe you regret that impulsive e-mail. You can't erase what you've written.

Perhaps hasty, thoughtless words blurted in anger strained a relationship or cost you a friendship. You can't suck your words back into your mouth. The ear that heard them can't just forget them.

Then there's hasty, impulsive buying. Whether it's clothes, shoes, gadgets, groceries, a car, a house or any number of things, when we don't guard our thinking process, we live to regret it.

Eating—did I mention eating? Yes, hasty eating, not thinking about the choices we're making, is a bad habit. The results speak for themselves. And eating too fast is bad for digestion.

Or maybe you made a hasty business decision you regret, such as co-signing a note for somebody, or going into business. Signing with the wrong company, you ended up in a financial hole.

Maybe you hurried to cut up vegetables for dinner and ended up cutting your finger. Then you had to clean your hand and bandage it before you could resume meal preparation. The time you tried to save by hurrying ended up hurting you physically (and costing you more time).

Any speeders out there? If you're always in a hurry, have the "pedal to the metal," you will likely end up paying a stiff fine, having your license revoked, or landing in jail. Maybe all three.

Haste makes waste! That waste brings embarrassment, loss of respect, loss of friendships, strained relationships, financial difficulties, physical pain and wasted time. God's word is wisdom for us, but we must take the time to read and obey it.

Can God redeem those "hasties" in our lives? Yes, He can bring something good out of our mistakes if we humble ourselves. We must go back to those we hurt and make amends, stop impulsive buying, eat right, and slow down. Joy awaits us through applying wisdom, and we'll do well to read and heed the wisdom found in the entire book of Proverbs.

Scriptures to Meditate:

- "He who is slow to wrath has great understanding, but he who is impulsive exalts folly" (Proverbs 14:29).
- "Also, it is not good to have zeal without knowledge, and he sins who hastens with his feet" (Proverbs 19:2).
- "The plans of the diligent lead surely to plenty, but those of everyone who is hasty, surely to poverty" (Proverbs 21:5).
- "A faithful man will abound with blessings, but he who hastens to be rich will not go unpunished" (Proverbs 28:20).

- "Do you see a man hasty in his words? There is more hope for a fool than for him" (Proverbs 29:20).
- "Do not be rash with your mouth and let not your heart utter anything hastily before God. For God is in heaven, and you are on earth; so let your words be few" (Ecclesiastes 5:2).
- So then, my beloved brethren, let every man be swift to hear, slow to speak, slow to wrath" (James 1:19).

Declare: I choose God's wisdom today!

Where have you been hasty, and it ended up costing you something? Ask God to redeem it.

_____

_____

52

Masks

According to Webster's Ninth New Collegiate Dictionary, the definition of a mask is "a pretense, a disguise, something that serves to conceal something from view; to take part in a masquerade."

There are all kinds of masks. Some, such as a painter's mask and a gas mask, protect us from harmful substances. Surgical masks protect against disease, and an oxygen mask is beneficial if needed. A ski mask protects the skier from harsh wind and cold, and a cosmetic mask nourishes facial skin. Other masks, such as a costume party mask, theatrical mask, Halloween mask or a witch doctor's mask, is what we usually think of as soon as the word "mask" is mentioned—something scary or grotesque to hide behind.

Then there is the human "poker face" mask, void of expression to hide our emotions or beliefs. Why do we wear emotional masks? I believe it's because of fear: fear of being ridiculed and rejected, or sometimes fear of incurring physical harm, as in abusive situations. Proverbs 27:19 says, "As in water face reflects face, so a man's heart reveals the man." Our feelings and thoughts register on our faces and in our body language.

A clichéd greeting in our society is, "How are you?" The expected standard answer is "Fine. How are you?" And then each moves on. I understand that we don't interact deeply with a fellow shopper or casual acquaintance, but what if we honestly said we're having a bad or blessed day? It might start a conversation that could open the door to minister the love of Jesus to someone. We are such creatures of habit, and it would be good for us to think about developing a genuine openness with people.

Even among our family, friends and church circles, too many of us put on a front, say "I'm fine," and hide our true feelings. It's like we close a door to any perceived threat. And sometimes with good reason. If we have been hurt and "stung" before, we are cautious and tentative. The result is that we close ourselves off from people and are crippled in our friendships. We create inner tension for ourselves as we hold in our feelings, which can result in sickness and disease.

It takes a conscious effort to allow oneself to trust again. But the benefits of allowing others to see the real "us" is that others will trust us to be honest and genuine. We'll also feel better physically and emotionally.

The flip side of the coin is this: emotional masks are not always bad. Wearing an emotional mask can protect us from inappropriate expressions of shock, disappointment, laughter or anger. I think of how a psychologist, counselor or pastor may have to be poker-faced to avoid alienating the person he's trying to help. In the Muslim world, a poker-faced mask and careful answers can save the life of a Muslim who's converted to Christianity. And there are many such Muslims, as described in the book, *Dreams and Visions: Is Jesus Awakening the Muslim World?* by Tom Doyle with Greg Webster.

We in the free world have no idea what goes on in those countries unless we read a book like the one I mentioned. We take our freedoms for granted. And really, compared to what our Christian brothers and sisters must endure in Muslim countries, we owe it to ourselves to get rid of our thin skin and fear of being judged by others. We need to take off our masks of fear and rigid control and be real with others. Let's unmask, open our hearts and speak the truth in love. Scary? Perhaps. But remember Philippians 4:13: "I can do all things through Christ Who strengthens me."

Scripture to Meditate:

- "Bear one another's burdens, and so fulfill the law of Christ" (Galatians 6:2).
- "But encourage one another daily, as long as it is called 'Today,' so that none of you may be hardened by sin's deceitfulness" (Hebrews 3:13, NIV).

How can you be more open with others?

_____

_____

53

Holidays and Relationships

Thanksgiving Day. The last family members had left after farewells and hugs were exchanged. Caroline tucked her hair behind her right ear and wiped a stray tear from her cheek as she put the last plate into the dishwasher. She added the detergent, clicked the door shut and pushed the start button. A persistent lump rose in her throat as she thought about past Thanksgivings. Why couldn't Clark just agree to disagree with Paul and Theresa? Why did they always end up in an argument? Last year, Paul and Theresa left without even saying "goodbye," and this year they had refused to come at all. If Clark would only call and apologize to them. . . If only Paul and Theresa wouldn't be so touchy and easily offended. . .

Do you look forward to holidays with your relatives? Or do you dread the scrutiny of Aunt Susie once again? Do you look for an excuse to avoid the family get-together? Maybe you haven't spoken to your brother for a long time because he hurt your feelings. Or perhaps you feel a parent has wronged you, and you don't plan to ever go home again for Thanksgiving. Christmas either, for that matter. Brother, sister, mother, father, grandfather, grandmother, cousin, aunt, uncle: does it matter who it is?

Grudges and ill will exist and persist in many families. And that's a shame, because the family unit should be a pleasant place of warmth and acceptance, love and forgiveness, peace and unity—not pain, hatred, heated arguments or strained silence. God knows there is enough pain out there in the world without getting a dose of it from your own family. So, you stay away. Yet your heart aches a bit more with each passing holiday as the chasm of separation widens.

I think of the Scripture in James 4:1 (NIV) that says, "What causes fights and quarrels among you? Don't they come from your desires that battle within you?" And Proverbs 18:19 declares, "A brother offended is harder to win than a strong city, and contentions are like the bars of a castle." We are all prone to self-interest and self-preservation. But God also tells us in Romans 12:18, "If it is possible, as much as depends on you, live peaceably with all men."

Good relationships take work and sometimes lots of prayer. Friendship and unity must be preserved, or they deteriorate. It takes soul-searching honesty and humility of heart to reach out in a strained relationship to bring restoration. Good communication skills are so vital! I heartily recommend the book, *Keep Your Love on* by Danny Silk. It contains a wealth of effective relationship tools.

Is God speaking to your heart about a difficult person in your family? Ask God what you can do to reach out to someone in your family and help restore peace and unity. Whether you were the one offended, or whether you offended someone, peace must start with you. Don't wait for the other person. The most spiritual person goes first, you know.

- Begin to thank God for each person in your family—even the difficult ones.
- Ask God to pour out His Spirit in his/her life.
- Ask God to give them wisdom and revelation for their life.
- Pray for their salvation if they are not born again.
- Ask God for a fresh baptism of love in your own heart for them.

- Ask yourself, "Have I contributed negatively to this strained relationship?"
- Ask God to show you what you can do to change that and reach out to them.
- Believe God is working in that person right now.
- Believe God is at work in you too!

Scripture to Mediate:

- "Blessed are the peacemakers, for they shall be called sons of God" (Matthew 5:9).
- "How good and pleasant it is when brothers live in unity!" (Psalm 133:1).

May all your holidays and relationships be the best ever! Write your thoughts/plans here.

_____

_____

54

From Anger to Prayer

Wednesday, November 7, 2012, was a dark day for me. A storm of strong emotions ripped at the fabric of my soul. The presidential election that announced Obama the winner left me stunned and incredulous. I felt burdened with deep anger, hurt, and grief. I felt betrayed by the three million Christians who refused to vote because they didn't like the other candidate's religion. Couldn't they see we weren't voting for a church pastor? Apparently not. I wondered if our nation had sunk so low as to deserve a president who openly approves of, and wants laws passed encouraging homosexuality, abortion, and disregard for our Constitution. A president whose current governing ideas I found highly offensive and destructive to our nation, homes, and families.

I thought of Scriptures like Psalm 55:11, "Destructive forces are at work in the city; threats and lies never leave its streets." And Psalm 12:8, "The wicked freely strut about when what is vile is honored among men." I thought of my pastor's recent comment in a sermon: "Christians massage the word of God to mold it to fit their personal preferences or beliefs." I felt betrayed by fellow believers in the Lord Jesus. Where were the disciples of the Lord Jesus?

All day I felt torn and tearful; but I knew I could not stay there. Instead, as a sacrifice of praise, I chose to turn my focus to the loveliness of Jesus instead of all the filth and disappointment in the world. I asked the Holy Spirit to help me praise Him in all circumstances.

Some days after the election, I read I Timothy 2:1 – 2 (NIV): "I urge, then, first of all, that requests, prayers, intercession and thanksgiving be made for everyone—for kings and all those in authority, that we may live peaceful and quiet lives in all godliness and holiness. This is good, and pleases God our Savior, who wants all men to be saved and to come to a knowledge of the truth."

I wondered, "How can I give thanks to God for Obama? For a leader who stands for all I am against?" I thought of Paul and his letter to Timothy, and imagined the Christians living in that day had a hard time giving thanks to God for Caesar, too. Yet the Lord Jesus asked them to do it. I struggled for a moment as I wondered how I could thank God for Obama and not betray my strongly-held convictions that were based on God's word.

But I took a deep breath and thanked God for President Obama. I chose to do it in obedience to my Commander in Chief in Heaven, not because I felt like it, but because I loved the One Who forgave me my sins, gave me eternal life and declared me righteous and holy.

God did not say I had to thank Him Obama was re-elected, for how he governs, for what he says, or for his beliefs. I needed to thank God for Obama as a person made in the image of God and respect the office of the presidency. God instituted levels of authority in government, so we'd have an orderly society.

I thanked God that He can turn our President Obama's heart to what is right. I prayed for his salvation and that of his family, and for his advisers. For each member of the House of Representatives and the Senate. The Supreme Court, and on down to the state and local levels. As Scripture says in Proverbs 21:1 that "The king's heart is in the hand of the Lord, like the rivers of water; He turns it wherever He wishes." And I stood in faith on that Scripture.

The very next day, we read a prophecy from someone we trust, that the Lord Jesus was grieved by our lack of prayer for Obama and the words spoken by the Church against him over the previous four years. We, the church, had tied His hands. The Lord could not do what He desired in our President. Our words matter in the earth and carry the power of life or death over people and circumstances.

The prophecy contained the same thing the Lord had shown me and my husband the night before, which was this: we need to believe God to give Barak Obama a new heart, new priorities, new vision, sanctified by the God of Heaven! We need to believe God to turn him into a godly president. I believed God to give President Obama dreams or visions in the night, that he would hear a voice say, "This is the way; walk in it." We need to obey God and give thanks for all those in authority over us. We need to cultivate an attitude of gratitude in all areas of life. I believed God could still give us a "new" president!

Our circumstances always provide plenty of opportunities to be ungrateful, down in the dumps, negative, and even downright nasty. I've thought about it, and I believe the antidote for the doldrums is the giving of thanks. The Word of God has much to say about giving thanks; the Psalms are full of praise and thanks to the Lord.

What I have found freeing is to make up my own little short songs to the Lord, rejoicing in Him, and giving Him thanks. There's something about thankfulness on our part toward God that frees His hand to work in our circumstances and answer our prayers. Yes, I'll say it again: giving thanks to God will kill anger.

Scripture to Meditate:

- "I urge, then, first of all, that requests, prayers, intercession and thanksgiving be made for everyone—for kings and all those in authority, that we may live peaceful and quiet lives in all godliness and holiness. This is good, and pleases God our Savior, who wants all men to be saved and to come to a knowledge of the truth" (I Timothy 2:1 – 2, NIV).
- "Do not repay evil with evil or insult with insult, but with blessing, because to this you were called so that you may inherit a blessing" (I Peter 3:9, NIV).

- "Rejoice always, pray without ceasing, in everything give thanks; for this is the will of God in Christ Jesus for you" (I Thessalonians 5:16 – 18).
- "As you therefore have received Christ Jesus the Lord, so walk in Him, rooted and built up in Him and established in the faith, as you have been taught, abounding in it with thanksgiving" (Colossians 2:7). You'll be pleasant company!
- "And let the peace of God rule in your hearts, to which also you were called in one body; and be thankful" (Colossians 3:15).

Who do you need to pray for today? Do you need to change your attitude?

_____

_____

55

What Do You Say?

Ecclesiastes 12:11 reads, "The words of the wise are like goads, and the words of scholars are like well-driven nails, given by one Shepherd." Someone once said, "Our words act as nails constructing things in the Spirit. Just as a nail is used to keep a board in place, words are used to keep God's promises in place, allowing them to build things in the Spirit."

There is a spiritual principle that we must know and believe, and we learn it from our Creator. Genesis 1:2 says, "The earth was without form, and void; and darkness was on the face of the deep. And the Spirit of God was hovering over the face of the waters. Then God said, 'Let there be light, and there was light.'" Wow. God created order and beauty out of chaos by speaking words! And He has put His power into words for us to use! What an amazing truth!

God said in Isaiah 55:10-11, "For as the rain comes down, and the snow from heaven, and do not return there, but water the earth, and make it bring forth and bud, that it may give seed to the sower and bread to the eater, so shall My word be that goes forth from My mouth; it shall not return to Me void, but it shall accomplish what I please, and it shall prosper in the thing for which I sent it."

Consider the amazing scripture in Romans 4:17b: "(God) calls those things which do not exist as though they did." God brings life to dead places by calling the things that aren't as though they were. He declares the end from the beginning.

Jesus' disciples were amazed that the fig tree Jesus cursed in Mark 11:13-14 had withered away and died by the next day. Consider Jesus' response to his disciples in Mark 11:22-24: "So Jesus answered and said to them, 'Have faith in God. For assuredly I say to you, whoever says to this mountain, "Be removed and be cast into the sea," and does not doubt in his heart, but believes that those things he says will be done, he will have whatever he says. Therefore, I say to you, whatever things you ask when you pray, believe that you receive them, and you will have them.'" Wow. What a promise! Praying is saying. And saying is praying when we do it in faith.

God has given us exceeding great and precious promises to speak! 2 Peter 1:3 – 4 explains, "His divine power has given to us all things that pertain to life and godliness through the knowledge of Him who called us by glory and virtue, by which have been given to us exceedingly great and precious promises, that through these you may be partakers of the divine nature, having escaped the corruption that is in the world through lust."

God wants mankind to rule and manage the earth for Him, as seen in Genesis 1:26 and 28, Psalm 8:6 – 8, and Psalm 115: 16. How are we to rule? We are to speak words of faith and authority, and take dominion over the devil's works of darkness. Jesus defeated him by His death and resurrection, but Satan tries to deceive us into believing he can still rule. And indeed, he can if we allow him to. That's why it's important to enforce his defeat. God plainly tells us that we can submit to Him, resist the devil, and he will flee from us (James 4:7). We do it by obeying God and speaking words of life over dead situations, trouble and disease.

Proverbs 18:21 says, "Death and life are in the power of the tongue, and those who love it will eat its fruit." We can speak either life or death, and the spiritual principle is that, sooner or later, our words will produce a harvest of the seed sown. Let's speak God's promises. You may ask,

"Well, what are they?" The word of God is filled with promises, and as we read the Bible, we will find those promises that become alive in our hearts. I have included some promises for you at the end of this book.

Much joy comes from standing on God promises. For example, I Peter 2:24 and Isaiah 53:5 tell us that "By Jesus' stripes we have been healed." That means physical healing. Make the word of God personal for you; put your name in verses where it says "we" or "our", and it becomes a promise to you. The Holy Spirit will cause certain verses to "leap out" at you; stand on those! Speak them out—declare them in faith, and don't give up. The enemy tries to discourage us, but we stand firm. Remember: death and life are in the power of the tongue!

Scripture to Meditate:

- "No man can tame the tongue; it is an unruly evil, full of deadly poison. With it we bless our God and Father, and with it we curse men, who have been made in the similitude of God. Out of the same mouth proceed blessing and cursing. My brethren, these things ought not to be so" (James 3:8 – 10).
- "Remind them to be subject to rulers and authorities, to obey, to be ready for every good work, to speak evil of no one, to be peaceable, gentle, showing all humility to all men" (Titus 3:1 – 2).
- "Let the words of my mouth and the meditation of my heart be acceptable in Your sight, O Lord, my strength and Redeemer" (Psalm 19:14)

What promise from God is especially meaningful to you?

_____

_____

56

Thanksgiving

Joy and thanksgiving rose in my heart as I lay in my warm bed with flannel sheets. My house was clean, the table was set, the turkey waited in the fridge for morning to arrive. And our family was coming for Thanksgiving Day. Suddenly, a feeling of guilt tried to crowd out my joy as I thought of the hungry and homeless. I felt like my thankfulness to God was snatched away by thoughts of guilt and condemnation as though I should not have a good life and nice things.

As I thought about it, I realized that feeling guilty would not feed or house those less fortunate. I truly prayed for them and asked God to send them help; and indeed, we have, many times, helped those in need. Guilt can truly be a contentment-snatcher. It pleased God that I was filled with thanksgiving for all His blessings, and it was right I should enjoy that warm, cozy feeling of gratitude, and not get hijacked by guilt.

Thankfulness can also be hijacked by "Black Friday," the day immediately following Thanksgiving Day that starts the Christmas shopping season. Images come to mind of people camping out in front of stores all night so they are the first ones inside the door to grab the latest gadget for huge savings. Images of people trampled and injured in the mad rush when the doors open at 7:00 a.m. Images of women fighting over one last doll; fists and angry voices raised as other fights break out. Images of anger and ill-will—just the opposite of what they supposedly celebrated the day before!

I think of the Scripture in James that says, "What causes fights and quarrels among you? Don't they come from your desires that battle within you? You want something but don't get it. You kill and covet, but you cannot have what you want. You quarrel and fight. You do not have, because you do not ask God. When you ask, you do not receive, because you ask with wrong motives, that you may spend what you get on your pleasures" (James 4:1, NIV).

I'm not saying it's wrong to participate in getting good deals on "Black Friday," but it is wrong to be discontent and greedy. Philippians 4:11 – 13 in the New International Version says, ". . . for I have learned to be content whatever the circumstances. I know what it is to be in need, and I know what it is to have plenty. I have learned the secret of being content in any and every situation, whether well fed or hungry, whether living in plenty or in want. I can do everything through him who gives me strength." That doesn't mean we never want to improve ourselves or have nice things. I like the Amplified Bible translation of verse eleven of the same reference: ". . .for I have learned how to be content (satisfied to the point where I am not disturbed or disquieted) in whatever state I am."

Let's look at I Timothy 6:6 – 10 in the NIV: "But godliness with contentment is great gain. For we brought nothing into the world, and we can take nothing out of it. But if we have food and clothing, we will be content with that. People who want to get rich fall into temptation and a trap and into many foolish and harmful desires that plunge men into ruin and destruction. For the love of money is the root of all kinds of evil. Some people, eager for money, have wandered from the faith and pierced themselves with many griefs."

I Timothy 6:17 – 18 in the NIV continues, "Command those who are rich in this present world not to be arrogant nor to put their hope in wealth, which is so uncertain, but to put their hope in God, who richly provides us with everything for our enjoyment. Command them to do good, to be rich in good deeds, and to be generous and willing to share."

Finally, let's rest in Hebrews 13:5 – 6, NIV: ". . . keep your lives free from the love of money and be content with what you have, because God has said, 'Never will I leave you; never will I forsake you.' So, we say with confidence, 'The Lord is my helper; I will not be afraid. What can man do to me?'"

A heart filled with thanksgiving will produce a life of contentment. Dear Reader, I bless you in Jesus' Name; may your life be one filled to overflowing with contentment by God's goodness, grace, and peace!

Tell God what are you especially thankful for today.

_____

_____

57

The Bait of Offense

Eloise was convinced Patty was mad at her for some unknown reason, because Patty walked right past her without saying "hello."

John and Theresa left their church because they felt lonely, unappreciated and overlooked.

Paula slept on the edge of the mattress because she felt Brian owed her a huge apology. Brian turned his back to her and went to sleep. Tears slid down Paula's cheeks and sleep refused to come, as angry thoughts ran laps through her mind.

Leslie was livid. Mary, with whom she had prayed and entrusted the secret of a painful affair in her past, told another friend, and now the whole church knew. She felt totally betrayed.

Clara looked wide-eyed at Lois. How had she lost all that weight? How dare she come around flaunting stiletto heels, dressed to the nines, sporting a new hairdo? How could she afford those clothes? Clara looked down at the lumps and bumps on her own overweight body and her three-year-old Christmas outfit. She fought back the tears as she thought of her husband's cut in pay and their financial struggles. Suddenly she just wanted to get out of there—leave the family Christmas gathering.

The spirit of offense is a terrible thing that can grow into a root of bitterness if not dealt with immediately. We can feel offended when people seem better off than we are, don't agree with us, overlook us or discount our accomplishments, are rude, mistreat us, etc. A spirit of offense causes people to feel wounded, misunderstood, hurt, angry, resentful, envious, and jealous. A spirit of offense makes you want to retaliate. A spirit of offense makes you blame others instead of looking at yourself. Makes you want to prove you're right. A spirit of offense causes one to misunderstand and wrongly judge another's motives. It's the spirit behind murders and school shootings, arson and violence of every sort. It's an evil spirit from the pit of hell itself.

Hebrews 12:15 tells us that we are to see to it that no one misses the grace of God and becomes defiled. What does it mean to miss the grace of God? Let me ask you: if we Christians understood how much God has forgiven us, would we refuse to forgive someone else? If we understood and believed that God approves of us, would we be offended, resentful, envious or jealous of someone else? If we understood that we are forgiven and cleansed of our sins, would we feel insecure? No, understanding and experiencing these truths would establish us in grace and make us a very thankful people.

If we are not established in grace, we'll take the bait in Satan's trap of offense. Consider that to snare an animal, a trapper must bait the trap to lure the creature. If we don't take the bait (entertain thoughts of offense), no harm will come to us. We must watch out for Satan's traps and not take his bait. The possibilities to be offended are as endless as the list of our relationships. The truth is, only those you care about can hurt you.

If we refuse to forgive or believe the best of others, a root of bitterness grows like a cancer. It destroys marriages and families, breaks up close friends, keeps people out of church, causes backsliding, inhibits or destroys our own God-given potential, topples businesses, and corrupts governments. It sucks the life and joy out of everything. The root of bitterness feeds on selfishness, and selfishness is the sin of pride in every human heart.

Consider that roots are the avenue of nutrition to feed what's above ground, that which is seen. Roots are hidden. A person can seem totally fine by all appearances but have deep roots of bitterness hidden inside. Sooner or later, the fruit will appear from the root. We must be rooted and grounded in love, as Ephesians 3:16 - 19 says.

Scripture to Meditate:

- "A brother offended is harder to win than a strong city, and contentions are like the bars of a castle" (Proverbs 18:19).
- "The discretion of a man makes him slow to anger, and his glory is to overlook a transgression" (Proverbs 19:11).
- "Walk worthy of the calling with which you were called, with all lowliness and gentleness, with longsuffering, bearing with one another in love, endeavoring to keep the unity of the Spirit in the bond of peace" (Ephesians 4:1 – 3).
- "So then, my beloved brethren, let every man be swift to hear, slow to speak, slow to wrath; for the wrath of man does not produce the righteousness of God" (James 1:19 – 20).
- Read James 4.
- "Looking carefully lest anyone fall short of the grace of God, lest any root of bitterness springing up cause trouble, and by this many become defiled" (Hebrews 12:15).

May God's grace produce the fruit of love that blossoms and grows in your home, family, and personal relationships. I bless you in Jesus' Name to that end!

Where do you need to guard against taking offense?

_____

_____

58

To Give or Not to Give?
That is the Question

Nancy*

She asked me to friend her on Facebook, so I did, but I didn't know her at all. About six months later, I got a private message telling me she has no food in her house, has two children, and had lost her job a couple months earlier. She said she lost both her father and her mother in the space of two years and neither she nor her husband had any friends. Her siblings were on drugs and incapable of helping anyone. She asked if I would help, because she felt like she could turn to me. I found her request quite odd and surprising, but my heart of compassion went out to her. My husband and I talked about it, and agreed we'd give her a check for fifty dollars to buy groceries. Throughout the next year, we often paid for some electric bills, more and more groceries and other expenses, and each time we struggled with, "Is this the right thing to do, or are we creating a state of dependency?" Nancy was always very grateful for our help.

I found out she didn't know how to cook, and had no cookware, so I bought her a set along with kitchen utensils; I wondered how she fed her husband and two children if she couldn't cook. I gave her a copy of my cookbook I had just published and showed her how to fix some food. I bought groceries for them myself once to make sure the money was going to feed her family, but it seemed every week or so there was a new financial crisis. She was also depressed, had heart health issues, and needed money for heart medication. We paid for several ministry counseling sessions at our church, which she said helped. Her husband had a low-paying job and didn't seem motivated to look for anything better, and Nancy said they had arguments, because she felt it was up to her to get help for the family.

One day I had a "girl's day out" with her, took her to lunch, went shopping for some new clothes, bought her some bed linens, pillows, a Bible, and other things she said she didn't have. I helped do job searches online for her, and she did get hired temporarily a couple of times, only to be fired. She wasn't happy there, wasn't treated well, she said. She missed her old job.

It finally got to the point where Dave and I said we couldn't keep doing this anymore. It isn't that we didn't have the money (and we had given them a lot), but we felt her husband had to step up and take responsibility for his own family.

To make a long story short, one day I had a heart-to-heart talk with her at my house and told her we couldn't be their lifeline anymore. It was hard for me to do that, but she understood. We kept praying for them, and she eventually got hired back at her old job, and they are doing well today. So, overall, I was glad we were able to help them get stabilized.

Paul *

Some years ago, I responded to a plea from Marcus Lamb, owner of Daystar TV, to write to a Christian prisoner he felt had been wrongly convicted. Soon his cell mate, Paul (also a Christian), asked that I write to him too. Paul was very appreciative, and from time to time we sent him good books from Amazon to strengthen his faith. After about two years, he asked us for an mp3 player, money for stamps, writing paper, coffee and whatever. We hesitated and only put twenty-five dollars into his account with the Federal Bureau of Prisons. It seemed that each time we gave, he asked for more. At one point he confessed to us that he had used some of the money for drugs and was terribly sorry. He said we have no idea how hard prison is, and (to make a long story short) eventually insisted we had to help him start a Bible study in prison by sending him one hundred dollars a month, or he "couldn't make it." We drew the line at that; he had "made it" for eight years in prison before he knew us; how come now he suddenly can't "make it" anymore?

Homeless woman

Several years ago, a homeless woman pushed her cart to block the driver's side of my car as I came out of a Christian bookstore. I felt resentful, because I knew she wanted money. I engaged her in conversation, and learned she was on the streets because of a family feud. I did feel sorry for her, and finally gave her a twenty-dollar bill before she moved her cart, so I could leave. I must say, I didn't feel too cheerful in my giving.

Darrell and Stephanie *

One winter day several years ago, I went to Food Lion and met a woman at the checkout buying a cup of coffee. I learned her husband was in the parking lot on his motorcycle, waiting on her. I also learned she and her husband were homeless. Oh, how I wanted to do something to help them, as I thought what it would be like to be out in the cold with no place to call home and get warm, take a shower, sleep, eat, etc. Until it was all said and done, over the course of several months, we gave them food, money, a couple of overnight stays in our home, one week in a hotel, money to get his bike fixed; we got his cell phone operational, and more. We finally had to put a stop to it, because it seemed the more we did for them, the more they wanted. I didn't feel like they were very grateful, either. Rather, they seemed to feel they were entitled to our help. We learned they were homeless because her mother wouldn't let them stay with her. We even tried to get them into a shelter, and Stephanie was willing, but her husband was not. He preferred to be homeless! We wondered if we had done right by them after all.

Have you ever been in a quandary about whether to give or not to give? How should Christians respond in situations like these? In a situation like Nancy's, it's a good idea to get them to meet with someone to work out a household budget and do work in exchange for money. In our case, we didn't have any work for either Nancy or her husband to do, but we did encourage them to meet with financial advisors at our church. Her husband was resistant, but they did come to church a few times. We are to be good stewards of our finances, and that includes being selective and prayerful in giving to organizations that request money through the mail. I like what I read somewhere: "Every situation of compassion has elements of wisdom. Ask questions before giving." Michael Spencer, British businessman and philanthropist said, "Stewardship is not just pure generosity. Generosity is an essential component, but it needs to be tempered by prudence, wisdom, and good judgment." Galatians 6:2 says we are to bear one another's burdens, and so fulfill the law of Christ. But then in verse five of the same chapter, God says "Each one shall bear his own load." I Thessalonians 5: 3 – 10 gives scriptural guidelines for widows who are in financial need.

Scripture to Meditate:

- "If there is among you a poor man of your brethren. . . you shall not harden your heart nor shut your hand from your poor brother, but you shall open your hand wide to him and willingly lend him sufficient for his need, whatever he needs. . .your heart shall not be grieved when you give to him, because for this thing the Lord your God will bless you in all your works and in all to which you put your hand. For the poor will never cease from the land; therefore, I command you saying, 'You shall open your hand wide to your brother, to your poor and your needy, in your land'" (Deuteronomy 15:7 – 11).

- "And just as you want men to do to you, you also do to them likewise" (Luke 6:31).
- "He who has pity on the poor lends to the Lord, and He will pay back what he has given" (Proverbs 19:17).
- "For even when we were with you, we commanded you this: if anyone will not work, neither shall he eat" (2 Thessalonians 3:10).
- "Laziness casts one into a deeps sleep, and an idle person will suffer hunger" (Proverbs 19:15).
- "Be wise as serpents and harmless as doves" (Matthew 10:16).
- "Get wisdom! Get understanding!" (Proverbs 4:5).
- "If any of you lacks wisdom, let him ask of God, who gives to all liberally and without reproach, and it will be given him" (James 1:5).

*Names have been changed

What do you believe about charitable giving?

_____

_____

59

Mothering Regrets

"You are not going to church dressed like that! Change into something dressier!" He resisted, and I persisted. My twelve-year-old son, Doug, was angry with me as I tried to dictate what he should wear. It finally came to the point of tears as we sat down on the couch together. I put my arm around him and told him I was sorry I'd spoken out of anger; he had tears too, and we made up. I realized I was more concerned about what people thought of me as a mother and the way my children dressed, than I was about the actual appropriateness of his attire, which was casual, but clean and neat.

As a mother, I deeply regret some things I did out of religious zeal because others said it was the right thing to do. But I had to remind myself that no woman, no mother is perfect, not even the ones that made it into the record of Scripture! As my children grew older, I had to learn:

- To relax my hold on them and let them make their own decisions. Our children must be responsible for their own actions; we can't make choices for them, much as we might like to sometimes.
- To pray much for my children; God can do more in ten seconds for them than we can do in a lifetime of trying to control them.
- Control drives them away from us.

- To teach them to seek what pleases God—not people.
- To give them freedom to have their own boundaries, to make their own mistakes, to say "yes," or "no," but love them no matter what. God gives us grace, and the goodness of God leads us to repentance, Scripture says. Trust God to work in their lives as He has worked in ours.
- To ask forgiveness of my child when I mess up in parenting.
- To tell God honestly what I did wrong and ask His forgiveness; Jesus' blood cleanses us from all sin by His blood at Calvary.
- To forgive myself for stupid things I've done. Forgiveness causes you to feel free and restored.

Sometimes we parents must forgive our children for ways they have hurt us, too. Forgiveness is a gift you give because it frees you. Someone once said, "Holding a grudge is like drinking poison and hoping your enemy dies." It is for freedom that Christ has set us free.

How do you deal with regrets in parenting? Dear one, whoever you are reading these words, be blessed with the freedom and joy that comes from knowing Jesus has forgiven all your sins and mistakes. Don't be so hard on yourself; sometimes we are our own worst enemy. God can redeem anything, and in all things, He works for our good if we belong to Him. He can even turn your mistakes around for good. God can unscramble an egg, untangle the strings of our lives. Take heart! Don't let the enemy, Satan, steal your joy, love and peace. God loves you unconditionally, without reservation. Believe it and be free from regrets! Don't mother them.

Declare:

"I give up my right today to hold *anything* against myself. I deserve to be punished, but Jesus took that punishment for me. I forget what lies behind and press on, moving forward in my life with God, even though I feel like I have blown it beyond repair. I reject this guilt and condemnation that the devil is trying to put on me. God is the God of second chances. I will no longer try to make myself feel bad to pay for what has been done. The price for my failures has been paid in full in Jesus' name!" (Gregory Dickow, pastor and Bible teacher)

Scripture to Meditate:

- "Who can find a virtuous wife? For her worth is far above rubies. . . She opens her mouth with wisdom, and on her tongue is the law of kindness. She watches over the ways of her household and does not eat the bread of idleness. Her children rise up and call her blessed; her husband also, and he praises her" (Proverbs 31:10, 26 – 28).
- Romans 8:1: "There is therefore now no condemnation to those who are in Christ Jesus, who do not walk according to the flesh (self-effort) but according to the Spirit. For the law of the Spirit of life in Christ Jesus has made me free from the law of sin and death" (Romans 8:1). (Brackets mine)
- ". . .but one thing I do, forgetting those things which are behind and reaching forward to those things which are ahead" (Philippians 3:13).

Write your thoughts here.

_____

_____

60

Renewing the Mind

We want to put our mental faculties to good use, and as Christians, we need to have our minds renewed to think and believe like Jesus. I Timothy 1:7 declares, "For God has not given us a spirit of fear, but of power and of love and of a sound mind." And I Corinthians 2:14 - 16 says, "The natural man does not receive the things of the Spirit of God, for they are foolishness to him, nor can he know them, because they are spiritually discerned. But he who is spiritual judges all things, yet he himself is rightly judged by no one. For who has known the mind of the Lord that we may instruct Him? But we have the mind of Christ." And the mind is the gateway to our soul and body.

We are made up of three parts: our spirit, our soul, and our body. Our spirit is made holy, righteous and totally perfect the moment we trust in Jesus' righteousness to save us. Now our soul (mind, will, and emotions) and our bodily appetites must be changed by the renewing of our minds to agree with our righteous spirit. Our new, made-righteous spirit is to be "boss" over our soul and body, and that takes time. We need to humble our minds to the word of God and receive instruction and wisdom and agree with the Word to renew our thinking. "For as he thinks in his heart, so is he" (Proverbs 23:7).

Just because we have trusted in Jesus for our salvation doesn't necessarily mean that our behavior automatically changes. We need to change our thinking, so it lines up with the word of God, as Romans 12:1 – 2 states: "Therefore, I urge you, brothers, in view of God's mercy, to offer your bodies as living sacrifices, holy and pleasing to God—this is your spiritual act of worship. Do not conform any longer to the pattern of this world but be transformed by the renewing of your mind" (NIV).

Deep scars and old patterns of coping with pain from a person's past need to be healed and changed by the power of the Holy Spirit. How wonderful that Jesus has given us His Word for healing, resting in His forgiveness and grace. Sometimes parts of the heart have crusted over so tightly with defenses to pain that it's difficult to let the love of God come in.

We renew our minds as we meditate on the Scriptures and agree with the Lord. I like to put my name in various places in the Psalms as I praise and worship the Lord. It's vital that we read the Word consistently and pray and allow God to be the plumb line for our lives. Our thinking needs to be changed and brought under the control of the Holy Spirit. How do we do that?

Part of meditating the word of God is repeating aloud what we read and claim the promises we find. His Word is like a gold mine: meditating and saying God's promises out loud causes new beliefs to form, and cements His truth in our heart. That's how we strengthen ourselves in the Lord, especially when we need help and comfort. I love to ask the Holy Spirit to minister His comfort to my heart when I need it, and He always does!

I highly recommend Wendy Backlund's excellent book, *Living from the Unseen: Reflections from a Transformed Life*. Her premise is that believing differently, not trying harder, is the key to change. I also highly recommend the devotional book, *Igniting Faith in 40 Days*, by Steve and Wendy Backlund.

Scripture to Meditate:

- "How can a young man cleanse his way? By giving heed according to Your word" (Psalm 119:9).
- "I say then: walk in the Spirit and you shall not fulfill the lust of the flesh" (Galatians 5:16).
- "You were taught, with regard to your former way of life, to put off your old self, which is being corrupted by its deceitful desires; to be made new in the attitude of your minds; and to put on the new self, created to be like God in true righteousness and holiness" (Ephesians 4:22 – 24).
- Read Ephesians 6:10 – 18.

Ask God to show you where your thinking needs to be renewed.

_____

_____

PSALM 91

He who dwells in the shelter of the Most High
Will rest in the shadow of the Almighty.
I will say of the Lord, "He is my refuge, and my fortress,
My God, in whom I trust."

Surely he will save you from the fowler's snare
And from the deadly pestilence.
He will cover you with his feathers,
And under his wings you will find refuge;
His faithfulness will be your shield and rampart.

You will not fear the terror of night,
Nor the arrow that flies by day,
Nor the pestilence that stalks in the darkness,
Nor the plague that destroys at midday.

A thousand may fall at your side,
Ten thousand at your right hand,
But it will not come near you.
You will only observe with your eyes
And see the punishment of the wicked.

If you make the Most High your dwelling –
Even the Lord, who is my refuge –
Then no harm will befall you,
No disaster will come near your tent.
For he will command His angels concerning you
To guard you in all your ways;
They will lift you up in their hands,
So that you will not strike your foot against a stone.
You will tread upon the lion and the cobra;
You will trample the great lion and the serpent.

"Because he loves me," says the Lord,
"I will rescue him; I will protect him, for he
Acknowledges my name.
He will call upon me, and I will answer him;
I will be with him in trouble,
I will deliver him and honor him.
With long life will I satisfy him
And show him my salvation."

(New International Version)

Scriptures and Declarations for Encouragement and Victory

"God always leads us in triumph in Christ Jesus!" 2 Corinthians 2:14

~

"Behold, I give you the authority to trample on serpents
and scorpions, and over all the power of the enemy, and
nothing shall by any means hurt you!" Luke 10:19

~

I have been given a spirit of power, love, and a
sound mind! (Based on 2 Timothy 1:7)

~

Faithful You are: faithful forever you will be! All Your promises
are "Yes" and "Amen!" (Based on 2 Corinthians 1:20)

~

Thank You, Jesus! You came to earth to give me abundant
life – until it overflows! (Based on John 10:10)

~

If believers drink any deadly thing, it will by no
means hurt them! (Based on Mark 16:18)

~

No evil shall befall me, nor shall any plague come
near my dwelling! (Based on Psalm 91:10)

~

Every cell in my body is full of life, health, and peace!

~

God has spoken, and He will make it good! God
keeps His promises! (Based on Numbers 23:19)

~

With long life the Lord satisfies me and shows
me His salvation! (Based on Psalm 91:16)

~

"Have faith in God. For assuredly I say to you, whoever says to
this mountain, 'Be removed and be cast into the sea, and does
not doubt in his heart, but believes that those things he says
will be done, he will have whatever he says." Mark 11:23

~

I declare the Word of God and believe I will have what I say; I forgive
those who have sinned against me. (Based on Mark 11:24-25)

~

"Surely, He has borne our griefs, sicknesses, weaknesses,
and distresses and pains. . . He was wounded for our
transgressions. . . and with the stripes that wounded Him we
are healed and made whole." (Isaiah 53:4-5, Amplified Bible)

~

By Jesus' wounds I have been made free and whole
from _____! (Based on I Peter 2:24)

~

In Christ, this _____ will not overwhelm me,
overcome me, overpower me, overthrow me, override me, overrule
me, overtake me, or overturn me! But I will overflow with abundant
life! I will go over the top and be above _____.

~

No weapon formed against me shall prosper, and every
tongue that rises against me in judgment I shall condemn.
This is my heritage in the Lord! (Based on Isaiah 54:17)

~

"God Himself has said, 'I will not in any way fail you nor give
you up nor leave you without support. I will not, I will not, I

will not in any degree leave you helpless nor forsake nor let you down (relax My hold on you)! (Hebrews 13:5, Amplified Bible)

"Fear not, for I am with you; be not dismayed, for I am your God. I will strengthen you, yes, I will help you, I will uphold you with My righteous right hand." (Isaiah 41:10)

I am: regenerated, re-energized, renewed, revitalized, re-established, restored and refreshed!

"He gives power to the weak, and to those who have no might He increases strength. . . Those who wait on the Lord shall renew their strength; they shall mount up with wings like eagles, they shall run and not be weary, they shall walk and not faint." (Isaiah 40:29-31)

Personal Note from the Author

When you are faced with challenges, I encourage you to put scriptures and declarations such as these on index cards and tape them where you can see them and declare them aloud regularly. I tape mine to the refrigerator, kitchen backsplash, dresser and bathroom mirrors. I continually speak the word of God throughout the day and encourage myself in the Lord by declaring Who He is to me, giving Him praise and worship even when I don't feel like it. I ask the Holy Spirit to help me, and He is such a faithful friend! The word of God is powerful and feeds your spirit as the Holy Spirit gives you revelation of His truth; the words we say from faith in our heart will produce a harvest, just like planting seeds in a garden produces a harvest of what is planted. Be encouraged: God is the author and finisher of your faith, and you're a winner!

God bless you richly, my friend!

Elaine

Printed in the United States
By Bookmasters